The Bullet

Also by Tom Lee

Greenfly: Stories
The Alarming Palsy of James Orr

The Bullet

A MEMOIR

Tom Lee

GRANTA

Granta Publications, 12 Addison Avenue, London W11 4QR

First published in Great Britain by Granta Books, 2024

Copyright © 2024 by Tom Lee

Tom Lee has asserted his moral right under the Copyright, Designs and Patents Act, 1988, to be identified as the author of this work.

Some of the material in the book has previously been published in the following pieces: 'The Creaking Door', *The Dublin Review*, Number 51, Summer 2013; 'The Invader and the Antidote', *The Dublin Review*, Number 57, Winter 2014–15; 'My Father's Asylum', *The Dublin Review*, Number 89, Winter 2022–23.

'Man and Wife' from *Collected Poems* by Robert Lowell. Copyright © 2003 by Harriet Lowell and Sheridan Lowell. Reprinted by permission of Farrar, Straus and Giroux. All rights reserved.

A CIP catalogue record for this book is available from the British Library.

9 8 7 6 5 4 3 2 1

ISBN 978 1 78378 504 9 (hardback)
ISBN 978 1 78378 506 3 (ebook)

Typeset in Galliard by Patty Rennie

Printed and bound by CPI Group (UK) Ltd, Croydon, CR0 4YY

www.granta.com

For Mum, Dad and Si

All night I've held your hand,
as if you had
a fourth time faced the kingdom of the mad –
its hackneyed speech, its homicidal eye –
and dragged me home alive...

Robert Lowell, 'Man and Wife'

Prologue

ONE AFTERNOON IN 2014 I DROVE UP TO THE OLD Severalls Hospital site just outside Colchester with my parents. I was recovering from a period of ill health and had been staying with them for the weekend to give my wife Ellie a break. I can't remember how the idea came up – perhaps my father had been telling his stories of being in hospital. Neither my mother nor my father had been there for nearly thirty years, and I was surprised when they suggested we go over and have a look. Since I had been ill, I had been asking more questions and this felt like an offering of sorts, an acknowledgement, a way into the past.

Severalls had opened in 1913 as the Second Essex County Lunatic Asylum, a large complex of buildings in the Queen Anne style set in extensive landscaped grounds, home at one time to as many as 2,000 patients. It was closed in the late 1990s as part of the general shutdown of dedicated psychiatric hospitals across the country and, with the exception of one or two of the smaller buildings repurposed for mainstream hospital services, the 300-acre site had stood derelict ever since. Barricaded behind fences and patrolled by dogs, the whole place off limits and going to ruin, it had become a magnet for kids and vandals and looters. 'Metal pirates' plundered lead from the roofs and copper from the mains wiring. There were frequent reports in the local press of trespassing and damage, and in 2005 the main hall, where dances had been held for the patients, was badly damaged by fire and had to be demolished.

It was a twenty-minute drive from my parents' house in a village on the other side of Colchester. The sign for the hospital was still there at the entrance, and we turned in and drove up the wide, oak-lined drive as far as the perimeter fence. Here there were warnings not to enter the site but there was no one around. We parked the car and let the dog out into the long grass.

My parents pointed things out to each other and to me, orientating themselves. By this time the hospital had been closed for many years and from our vantage behind the fence there wasn't much to see. There were several long, narrow, two-storey buildings that my mother thought had been hospital wards, the 'villas' that sat around the grounds away from the main building. The ground-floor windows were boarded up but on the first floor they were gaping open, glassless, and I could see straight through them and out of the windows on the other side to the sky beyond. The masonry was cracked, stained with damp and streaks of some kind of vegetative slime and covered in graffiti. The pitched roofs were heavily perforated, the timbering exposed – perhaps every other tile had come loose and fallen away.

It was a strange pilgrimage. My parents seemed relaxed enough, perhaps pleased to have outlived the place and see it abandoned, but I wondered at the layers of memory and feeling underneath. Perhaps the visit felt more significant to me than to them, given my state of mind at that time, but something had been triggered. I threw a ball for the dog. She saw a squirrel and chased it until it escaped up a tree. After a few minutes, we got back in the car and drove home.

PART ONE

Kingdom of the mad

SEVERALLS HOSPITAL, COLCHESTER, ESSEX

I

FOR ME, IT BEGAN IN THE SPRING OF 2008 AT A conference in Ireland. I was lonely and the town where I was staying was dismal and it rained. On the third day a fierce headache tightened across my temples until I had to go back to my hotel room and lie down. By the evening it had faded but I was exhausted and went to bed early. The next morning I woke at five, nauseous, with an odd stiffness in my hands. I took paracetamol, which seemed to help a little, struggled through the final conference session and then flew back to London.

The next day I still didn't feel well. My hands were so stiff that I couldn't hold a pen, and I phoned in sick to work. I had a hot bath and when I got out the parts of my body that had been in the water were covered in raised, red welts, each one as big as the palm of my hand. Over the phone my mother said I had once had something similar as a baby, something viral she had thought at the time. The welts went down but over the next few days I didn't feel any better. I slept badly, my body aching all over, as if I had flu. The nausea was continuous, and the only thing I could bring myself to eat were bananas, half a banana at a time. When Ellie got home from work, she found the uneaten halves all over the flat.

Over the next two weeks, the symptoms came and went. For a day or two my appetite returned, I had more energy and I began to think about going back to work; then the symptoms came back. It was a bad time to be ill. The day before I went to Ireland we had moved into a rented flat near the house we had bought in south London. The house was a wreck and builders were gutting and redecorating it before we could move in. The rented place was small and dark and cluttered with our moving boxes. Our daughter, then just over a year old, was underweight and not sleeping.

I began to worry that I would not recover from whatever this illness was. My thoughts circled continually around an image of myself as feeble, bedridden, housebound, unable to grasp onto the swirling responsibilities of my life – parenthood, work, moving house. At the end of my third week off work I was lying on the sofa in the middle of the night, unable to sleep, when these fears gripped me completely, apocalyptically. Looking back, I think of this as the moment when the true nature of what was happening to me revealed itself. It was as if all the physical symptoms of the past weeks had been a kind of phoney war going on inside me, the pre-tremors of a coming earthquake. I knew, suddenly, that I was very unwell, but not in the way I had supposed. I woke Ellie. I told her I was going mad and that I needed to be taken to hospital.

She took me to the doctor's surgery instead. I shook and wept whilst she explained to the GP what had been happening. The doctor diagnosed me with acute anxiety. She gave me a prescription for a week's worth of sleeping pills and for citalopram, an antidepressant that, she said, would probably begin to ease the anxiety after three or four weeks. I couldn't imagine how I would cope until then. It seemed intolerable that I would have to go on feeling this way for even a few more hours.

'Isn't there something that can help me now?' I said.

The doctor shook her head. 'I'm afraid not.'

It is impossible, I think, to describe what this kind of anxiety feels like, to properly convey it, to anyone who has not experienced it. The best way I can put it is that during that time it was as if I had *forgotten how to be.* By this I mean that every passing moment was unbearably intense and distressing. I felt that some internal switch had been flicked or shorted, leaving my body and mind in a state of unrelenting and unsolvable emergency.

The sleeping pills knocked me out for a few hours every night but I woke up at four or five every morning, exhausted, with the anxiety at full pitch the instant I became aware of myself. Even the smallest action, making a cup of tea or cleaning my teeth, was fraught with difficulty. I could not look after my daughter but I couldn't bear to be alone either, so on the days when Ellie had to go to work she dropped her off at my parents-in-law, and other people were timetabled to come over and be with me. My brother took time off work and came; other friends came. When I was very bad I stayed in bed and asked my visitors to sit or lie next to me. One friend, who was free to visit because he had just lost his job, did not want to sit on the bed. He brought a chair from another room but left after an hour. Only later did I see how alarming it must have been, how uncomfortable – for him and for everyone else – to see how utterly changed I was, how awkward for them to sit there in my stuffy sick room whilst I cried and apologised for the way I was, how much this friend, who had his own worries after all, had wanted to get away.

My anxiety cycled relentlessly through the same themes: that I would be sick for years; that I would lose my job; that I would never have the clarity of mind to write again; that I would never be able to look after my daughter or have another child; that Ellie would leave me or send me away; that my incurable anxiety would cause all these things to happen. At other times the anxiety detached itself from these specifics entirely and simply became the thing itself. This was anxiety in its purest, most concentrated form, an abstraction with almost no relation to the world around me, as rampant and absolute when I looked out of the window and watched a boy kicking a ball against a wall as it was each time I phoned work to say I would not be coming in.

I hung on desperately to the hope that the citalopram would work. Each day I took the drug was one day closer to the three or four weeks when this feeling might begin to be relieved. I was terrified, however, of what else the tablets might do to me and this became a toxic new strand to my anxiety. The doctor had said the drug could cause nausea, could make me feel worse before I felt better. Google searches confirmed this and much more. There were infinite numbers of forums and chatrooms where anxious, depressed people reported violent physical side effects, psychotic episodes and suicide attempts as a result of taking citalopram. It seemed entirely possible – probable even – that it was now the pills themselves that were making me ill, and every time I bent the packet and popped a pill out of its blister I braced myself as if I was swallowing a poison.

I spoke to my mother several times a day on the phone. When she came to visit she lay on the bed with me, put her arms around me and held my hand. She talked to me constantly, reassuring me, reminding me of things from my childhood. She talked about a family holiday when she and I had walked around Ullswater in the Lake District and my father and brother had rowed across the lake to meet us. The weather was beautiful and my brother and I were trying to persuade our parents to get a dog. Later on, we met my grandparents for tea. 'That was a happy day,' she said to me, over and over again, like a mantra, an incantation, 'that was a happy day.'

Around this time, two weeks or so after I had started on the citalopram, my friend Chris visited me. The day he came I was in a wretched state. I had not slept at all the night before and was so exhausted that I found it difficult to get around the flat. Chris tried to persuade me to take an Ativan, a benzodiazepine tranquillizer he was prescribed himself for anxiety. He was a good deal older than me and had been taking these pills for decades. He said it would help me rest but I was reluctant. I felt I was taking too many pills already – paracetamol, sleeping pills, the citalopram. I had not eaten since the day before and was sure that anything I took now, on an empty stomach, would make me sick. On top of all this, Ativan had not been prescribed to me, presumably for a reason. In the end, my desperation outweighed my fear. I sat up in bed and ate a little yoghurt to line my stomach. Chris broke the pill in two and gave me half.

After thirty minutes I felt no different, so I took the other half. Thirty minutes after that I got out of bed and went into the kitchen. The physical symptoms that had been afflicting me had evaporated entirely. The nausea had gone, so I made myself a sandwich and ate it sitting at the kitchen table with Chris. The stiffness in my hands had faded away. I had strength and energy. I felt mellow, but not dozy – alert, clear-headed, my thoughts no longer running into and climbing on top of each other. The feeling lasted for the rest of the afternoon and evening. It was miraculous. When Ellie returned with my daughter I played with her in the garden. Later on, I ate another meal which Ellie made and we watched TV together.

Chris left me with a strip of pills, ten in total. 'Make them last,' he said, 'it's not an endless supply.' Over the following weeks I took one from time to time, not every day, but whenever I could not cope and needed a break. I was uneasy. I had begun to read online about the dangers of benzodiazepine addiction and withdrawal, but I told myself that it was only a stopgap until the citalopram began to work. The websites seemed to agree that there was little risk of addiction if you took benzodiazepines for less than three weeks.

Each time I took one the effect was the same. I felt an immediate relief, the sure knowledge that in a few minutes the world would take on a far better shape. Within an hour I was transformed, restored to myself. I felt my thoughts settle and begin to focus. The terror of how to get through the rest of the day and those after it started to fade, and I could think about things I needed to do, now and in the future. The pill – this tiny, pale blue, slightly chalky, bevelled oblong, grooved down the middle to make it easier to break in two – seemed a perfect antidote to what I was suffering.

By then it was a very hot summer, and the neighbours whose garden backed onto our own barbecued in the afternoons, played loud house music and became rowdy. There were several days when, after taking an Ativan, I went out and lay in the garden in the sun. I tried to read the newspaper for a while as I waited for the pill to take effect. Then I closed my eyes, listened to the neighbours talking on the other side of the fence and let the beat of their music carry me along.

2

FOLLOWING THE VISIT TO THE SEVERALLS HOSPITAL site with my parents, I started browsing websites and online forums dedicated to illicit entry into the old asylums. These self-styled 'urban explorers' bag them like mountain tops, and Severalls featured prominently. Many of these explorers took their responsibilities seriously. There are meticulous, detailed descriptions of the buildings and their contents. This careful documenting, one website says, is all part of 'an obligation to the hospital's former inhabitants', whose temporary – or sometimes permanent – home was deserving of 'enormous attention and respect'. The explorers exchange information about security arrangements and how to evade them, stories of trips made, near misses and sometimes injuries sustained. One describes being caught at Severalls then led off the site by a friendly security man who filled him in on aspects of the hospital's history. There are other interested parties with an online presence, too: amateur naturalists interested in the bird and mammal life that has established itself amongst the decaying buildings, and ghost hunters.

The websites carry photos of Severalls' interior: rooms and corridors of peeling wallpaper, cracked plaster, stripped floors, colours that have run or turned fungal, bent light fittings, upturned desks and bed frames, and plant life pressed up against the windows or climbing in through broken or non-existent glass. There is graffiti everywhere. 'My Wounds Cry for the Grave' reads one message sprayed on a wall. 'LET ME OUT!' is another; intruders channelling what they believe to be the spirit of the old institution and its residents. In other rooms, clinical equipment has been pulled apart or pulled over – what looks like an ECT machine, a body refrigerator in the mortuary. The sense is of a place abandoned hastily and chaotically, without coordination, like some once-thriving civilisation abruptly and mysteriously vacated, or a shipwreck decaying on the seabed.

So evocative are these photos that a lushly produced spread made it into the *Daily Mail*, alongside sensational captions. 'Severalls Hospital seems to whisper with its own chilling history,' reads one, a place where 'psychiatrists were once free to test their new treatments without any restrictions on patients'. Many of the photos do have a kind of beauty – the ruined colours and textures; the authentic sense of entropy and a hidden world; artfully caught reflections in rainwater puddles on the floor; the woozy, submarine light. Some of them even feel staged – and perhaps they are. A chair, stripped to its frame, set at an angle to the large bay window in a derelict, high-ceilinged room, sunlight penetrating the ivy-covered window and pooling where a resident might once, we inevitably think, have sat and gazed out, with who knows what thoughts in their head. Overall, the effect is pleasing, the note of past trauma and suffering more or less anaesthetised and aestheticised, historic mental health care made to glow with a sense of nostalgia and distressed, vintage chic.

The Second Essex County Lunatic Asylum was one of the last of its kind to be built, at the tail end of the great wave of Victorian and Edwardian mental health reform. Prior to the 19th century, so-called lunatics tended to be regarded as subhuman, something other, afflicted by demonic or bestial forces. They ended up in workhouses or in the few grim and unregulated state and private asylums, often subject to brutal treatment: chains, whipping, total confinement, bloodletting, purging. Sometimes, as at Bethlem in London, they were put on show to generate income for the institution and provide entertainment to the sane.

In the early 19th century mental disorders gradually came to be seen as diseases of the brain, an affliction that anyone might fall prey to. William Tuke at the York Retreat and Phillipe Pinel in Paris pioneered the principle of 'moral treatment', the notion that humane care, the pursuit of normal life under favourable conditions, was the best means of exorcising morbid feelings and restoring the mentally unwell to health. In 1837 the reformer Dr William Browne, superintendent of the Montrose Lunatic Asylum in Scotland, wrote that the ideal asylum would be beautiful and open, with complete freedom inside its walls: 'There is in this community no compulsion, no chains, no whips, no corporal chastisement, simply because these are proved to be less effectual.' The main building would be a mansion, 'airy, and elevated, and elegant, surrounded by swelling grounds and gardens', containing 'galleries, and workshops, and music rooms', a 'hive of industry', with the lunatic residents 'weaving, baking, playing music, reading, drawing and bookbinding'. In 1845 the Lunacy Act made it compulsory for all counties and boroughs to provide asylums and brought them under the inspection of the Lunacy Commission. Over the next decades public asylums were built across the UK, and by 1914 there were more than 100,000 lunatics resident in over 100 institutions, around 0.6 per cent of the total population. For comparison, UK prisons currently hold just over 0.1 per cent of the population. It was a revolution, or, as Michel Foucault described this trend throughout Europe, the period of 'the Great Confinement'.

By 1900, the First Essex County Asylum at Brentwood had become critically overcrowded and a location was being sought for a new institution. The Board of Control – the rebranded Lunacy Commission – specified that the site for the new asylum be 'elevated, undulating in its surface, cheerful in its position, and having a general fall to the south or south-east', whilst also affording 'an uninterrupted view of surrounding country and free access of sun, and air'. The suggestion by a local alderman that a large hotel in Southend might be suitable for this purpose was dismissed, and instead the search was focused in the north of the county, which was flat, windswept and largely agricultural, with widespread poverty, unemployment and homelessness. In Colchester itself, a garrison town with a population of around 40,000 at the time, a shoemaking company employing 1,000 people had recently collapsed, resulting in economic conditions that typically created a large population of lunatics.

On the northern edge of Colchester, beyond the reach of public transport, a site was finally identified. The area had been woodland in the Middle Ages, then in the 17th century the location of a house or an inn called 'The Half Moon', and in the 18th century another inn, 'The Spread Eagle'. In 1903 Colchester Corporation agreed to sell 295 acres of the estate for £10,000, an area which included Cuckoo Farm. A temporary railway line was built from Colchester North station to carry building materials to the site.

A black and white aerial photograph of the finished asylum shows the sheer scale of the place – a sprawling palace or fortress town ringed by trees and fields – built at a total cost of £188,350. In May 1913, before its first residents arrived, it was opened to the public for three days. It was an event. Nearly 6,000 people came and it would have been hard for these visitors not to be impressed by the ambition of the enterprise, and perhaps a little astonished at the investment. It had the appearance, noted one, of 'a well-furnished hotel, calculated to give luxury and comfort to the inmates', in fact, 'so beautiful as almost to make a man himself a lunatic'. The main building was spread over fourteen acres and was 1,500 feet from east to west and 800 feet north to south. Inside, it was divided in two by a corridor that ran along its full length, at that time said to be the longest corridor in Europe, with male residents to the right of it and female residents to the left, a separation that was considered crucial to maintaining the moral health of the institution.

On the men's side were workshops where patients would be kept occupied and productive: tailoring, upholstering, cobbling, painting, carpentry, plumbing and glazing. On the women's side was a huge kitchen, a bakehouse, the laundry and a workshop for lunatic needlewomen. The wards contained small gardens or 'airing courts' where patients not fit to roam the wider site unsupervised could be exercised and receive the benefits of the bucolic setting. These allowed uninterrupted views of the rest of the grounds and the countryside beyond, and gave the impression of freedom, but were in fact bordered by ha-has, iron railings concealed in twelve-foot ditches. Between the two wings, and enclosed by the corridor, were the offices of the all-powerful physician superintendent, the other doctors and the nurses, as well as the stores and the main hall. All the wards in the main building were connected by a network of further corridors, roofed over but open to the elements at the sides. In later years, nurses would ride up and down them on bicycles.

The rest of the hospital buildings were scattered around the site in the newly fashionable villa system, making the most of the parkland, which had been extensively planted with trees and shrubs. On the south side was a large cricket ground. At the north-east corner of the site was the water tower, 100 feet high and visible from the centre of Colchester, the distinguishing architectural feature of this generation of asylums. A borehole sunk 400 feet into the ground provided fresh water. From the start, the asylum generated its own electricity and grew much of its own food on a farm within the grounds in an effort to be self-sufficient. The physician superintendent had his own house there and the nurses and many of the other staff were also resident. The whole site was surrounded by six-foot-high oak palings, with a deep trench on the outer side, and the wrought iron gates at the eastern end were the only access in and out. The asylum was to accommodate 1,500 lunatics at first, growing to 2,000 in the longer term. From its inception, it was designed to be a complete community, or what Erving Goffman would later call, less happily, 'a total institution'.

There were high ideals embodied in the design and location of the new asylum in Essex but, in truth, the vision and faith of the 19th-century mental health reformers had long since unravelled. Colney Hatch in north London opened with great fanfare in 1851 as the new Middlesex County Pauper Lunatic Asylum – later Friern Hospital – with a baroque facade, towers and cupolas. 'No Hand or Foot Will Be Bound Here' was emblazoned across the pediment of the main building. A year later the Lunacy Commission reported concerns about overcrowding and sanitation. By 1865 the patient population was twice its original capacity, restraints were in use and many of the ideals of 'moral treatment' were out the window. The Commission wrote, 'It would be difficult to instance more perfect examples of what the wards of an asylum... should not be, than are presented here.' *The Lancet* called Colney Hatch 'a colossal mistake' and there were calls for it to be closed.

The early successes of reformers like Tuke and Pinel had

proved difficult to replicate. They had depended in part on the zealous commitment of these individuals to their own institutions. John Conolly, resident physician at Hanwell Asylum in London, led the influential 'non-restraint movement' and during his tenure the number of patients at Hanwell doubled from its planned capacity of 500. He began to propose an ever-expanding list of the people he believed could benefit from the ideal society of the asylum – the eccentric, the unhygienic, the drunk, the dishonest, the ill-tempered, the disobedient. In time, Conolly himself developed a skin condition and insomnia and spent each night walking the halls and wards of the asylum before he was eventually forced into retirement. Overcrowding and stretched resources, amongst other things, made the principles of moral treatment hard to maintain in the now extensive network of asylums across the country. Rates of remission were low and so numbers of patients grew even further. As at Colney Hatch, straitjacketing and other forms of restraint were brought back and asylums once again became more custodial than therapeutic. The word 'asylum' alone carried a kind of toxic freight, almost the precise opposite of its original meaning, now indicative of a kind of secular hell.

The three-day ceremonial exposure of the new Second Essex County Lunatic Asylum to the public in 1913 was no doubt intended to revive some of the earlier spirit of reformist optimism. However, once the VIPs, local dignitaries and curious members of the public streamed out and the gates clanged shut behind them, it became, to a large extent, a closed world. For a little while, it continued to be the subject of local discussion, mainly concerning its cost. The county council was accused in the press of extravagance, particularly in relation to the building of a chapel for £10,000, apparently 'striving to imbue lunatics with the true principles of gothic architecture' and provide a 'place where lunatics could worship Him of whom they knew very little'. It was asked, predictably, whether the Lunacy Commission, the county council and Colchester Corporation should themselves be 'mentally examined'.

Once this petered out, however, with the exception of a German bombing raid in August 1942 which killed thirty-eight patients in the west wing of the hospital, the asylum was rarely mentioned in the local press for the next fifty years, an absence which seemed to reflect a wider official or public silence. Whether this was out of some unspoken taboo about the function of the place, the desire to keep such things and people out of plain sight, or because there was nothing to report, or some combination of these, it does not seem possible to say. The six-foot fence, the deep trench and the iron gates kept some people in and others out. The asylum was at a distance from Colchester itself and was not connected by public transport until a bus route was opened in 1930. It was official policy to recruit nurses from outside Essex as far as was possible in order to maintain a level of discretion around patients' identities and hospital affairs. Local people entered as patients but once certified as insane it was very difficult to be uncertified, and in most cases they never left. It is hardly surprising, then, that the asylum – like asylums all around the country – obscurely visible from the town but lurking mainly off camera, shrouded in secrecy and rumour, would acquire a forceful aura of existential dread. It became a place, according to author Diana Gittins, 'little known or understood, though much feared, where each and every individual might, if they were not careful, or if luck failed them, end up'.

3

TWO THOUSAND AND EIGHT, THE YEAR I BECAME
ill, should have been a good time in my life. Ellie and I were
due to get married, we were new parents, we had bought a
house and my first book was being published the following
year. But for that whole summer I was in freefall. I'd always
known that there was depression and anxiety in my family
but after thirty-five years of uneventful mental health I'd
felt I had 'dodged that bullet', as I told my mother when
she came to visit. Now, however, as I looked back over my
earlier life, it didn't seem so straightforward.

The summer I left university, in 1997, I had begun to
feel unwell. I was always exhausted. I had a constant sore
throat and headaches that went on for days and my mind
was often foggy, dulled. I was checked for everything and
I saw everyone. My GP ran tests for anaemia, diabetes,
glandular fever, allergies, Lyme disease, HIV and more. I
went to the hospital for a barium meal to see if there was
an issue with my digestion. I was desperate and getting
nowhere with the doctors, so I began to spend a fortune

on alternative therapists. I saw homeopaths, nutritionists, hypnotists, Reiki healers. Each one was confident that their treatment would bring me relief, and there was an appealing logic to the idea that my symptoms – undramatic, not obviously life-threatening, none of them visible, apparently not diagnosable in the conventional way, that came and went without evident relation to external factors – were the result of some subtle misalignment or blockage in my energies that might easily be tweaked to restore my physical equilibrium. It was possible to believe all sorts of things. Nothing worked. When my acupuncturist felt she was making no progress she referred me to her mentor, and he interviewed me about my symptoms in front of a lecture theatre of trainees who discussed the enigma of my case and took turns drawing my tongue.

Eventually, when I was twenty-five, a consultant at Barts Hospital diagnosed me with chronic fatigue syndrome. However, this brought little hope of treatment except a handful of sessions of cognitive behavioural therapy. The therapist was not much older than I was, a little nervous, and did not seem to know what to do with me. I sensed he had a theory, and at the second or third session he suggested that many chronic fatigue sufferers fitted a particular type – academic high achievers, burdened with high parental expectations, who could no longer live up to the pressure of these standards. I told him this didn't really fit, and anyway I did not like this emphasis on psychology. I stopped going to the sessions.

I read up on the syndrome but did not find it a useful

diagnosis. There was no agreement about what caused it, whether it was one or many things, or, at that time, if it even existed at all. Although I seemed to be at the mild end of the spectrum, the prognosis for sufferers was generally not good: years of, or perhaps even permanent, debilitation with little that could reliably be done to improve the situation. I was struggling at work and when my contract came to an end I left London and went to South America for six months, where I felt no different. It came in cycles – periods of days or weeks when I did feel better, almost fine – and my hopes would rise that the whole thing, whatever it was, had passed as mysteriously as it had come. Then a new cycle would begin and my optimism would be dashed. The cumulative effect of this, of so often feeling unwell, of not being able to escape this cycle, was overwhelming, defining, corrosive. I formed a picture of myself as disadvantaged compared to most other people I knew, of being limited by my health for who knew how long, perhaps for ever. It seemed that my body's natural state, the one to which it was constitutionally wired to return, was not that of health but of ill health, that feeling well was the aberration rather than the norm.

Before the emergence of chronic fatigue syndrome as a clinical category (originally and still sometimes known as myalgic encephalomyelitis or ME), the same collection of symptoms and absence of clear organic causes often resulted in a diagnosis of neurosis, neurasthenia, hypochondria or hysteria. In this interpretation, physical symptoms were the result of somatised emotional or psychological distress. I resisted this explanation for what I was feeling but at times, when I read the accounts and language of 19th- and early-20th-century neurasthenics, the sense of recognition was uncanny.

By this time, judging myself too unwell to cope with a conventional job and fearful for the future, I had signed on the dole and started to write seriously. At least, as a writer, there were countless models for sickliness, whether tubercular, drug-addicted or mentally unstable, even providing a veneer of romance and validation to the experience of being ill. Marcel Proust, perhaps the most iconic writer in this tradition, nearly killed by asthma as a child, retreated into his cork-lined bedroom on Boulevard Haussmann to protect himself from the smells and noises that caused him so much suffering. For myself, between joyless and unproductive writing sessions, I took long, groggy naps and frequent, morose walks around the park. In the evenings I lay in boiling hot, energy-sapping baths. Along with the appointments with various therapists, I took the homeopathic remedies, Chinese herbs and nutritional supplements that had been recommended to me, began diets that cut out one thing or another, stopped drinking alcohol and eliminated caffeine entirely, and tried yoga, Pilates and the Alexander Technique.

I did sometimes wonder if there were psychological issues at play. There was the family history, of course, and the question of how that might have affected me. I'd had a falling out with a friend and for a brief time I wondered whether the bad blood was somehow making me ill. I could see, too, that the lifestyle and work I was now pursuing were unlikely to be good for my mental wellbeing – the lack of structure, the requirement for solitary brooding, the high potential for a financial and professional dead end, the self-imposed pressure, the sense of gathering personal failure. I was stressed and unhappy, but these seemed clearly to be symptoms of my illness and the circumstances it imposed, rather than the other way around. I did not feel like a hysteric. I felt very sane, just madly frustrated and dismayed at my body's failure to operate properly. If my problems were psychological in origin, it was not in any way that I had previously understood the term.

Nevertheless, over the next few years I steadily got better. There was no new diagnosis or revelatory cure, just the gradual realisation that I was no longer defined by these symptoms and how they made me feel. I stopped spending money on therapists or experimenting with diets or exercise plans. I stopped signing on and instead took undemanding jobs that allowed me to concentrate on writing. I started to publish some stories. In 2005 I got a grant to finish a collection and Ellie and I went to Australia for six months to travel and write.

Around this time, six months or so after he retired, my father became ill with a flu-like virus that he could not shake off. Weeks turned to months and he began to give up learning French and playing the piano, hobbies that had been part of his retirement plan. It happened incrementally. He began to spend much of the day in bed. Then he set up a bed in the study on the ground floor to save the energy it took to climb the stairs. At first he came out for meals but then my mother started taking them in to him and he sat up at the desk to eat. He had a bucket and a cloth by the side of the bed to wash himself with. He got a wheelchair, and my mother – or my brother or I if we were visiting – wheeled him the few metres down the hall to the toilet or to sit for a little while in the living room, the conservatory or the garden, and then back to his sick room. He didn't have the concentration to read, so when he wasn't sleeping he lay in bed and listened to the radio.

He saw consultants and was diagnosed with chronic fatigue syndrome. Despite my doubts about my own diagnosis, I wondered, could not help wondering, about some family susceptibility to this particular illness. My parents must have considered this, too, but we did not speak about it. My father's case was much more acute than my own. For the first year or so there was the hope that it would pass soon enough and all plans and activities could be resumed. But gradually, as time went on and my parents' life was reshaped around the reality of his condition, it became normalised, less like a temporary situation than the status quo, the present and the future. He went on disability benefit and after two years they had a stairlift installed so that he could get upstairs to have a shower or bath. The timing of his illness seemed particularly cruel, though perhaps not unrelated. When I was growing up my father had worked non-stop, gradually colonising every room of the house with his books and papers. Retirement offered the opportunity to do different things, to pursue new interests. He had always wanted to travel more and there had been talk of a teaching job in Tanzania at a school a friend of his had set up. Instead, within a year he had been invalided. It is a curious, agonising, psychologically brutal way in which to be ill. There is nothing identifiable, nothing visible, nothing measurable, no proof of it except how you *feel*, no clear arc or threat of death, just a gradual narrowing of horizons, a chipping away at the terms of your existence. Despite this, my father was stoic and philosophical, almost as if one of the compensatory gifts of the illness was a remarkable resilience for dealing with it, rooting his hopes in the odd better day or week, the possibility of trying some new therapy or treatment.

To me, it seemed too much to bear. The interminable days punctured only by sleeping and meals and trips to the toilet, sitting for a while in another room or the garden, a kind of void or living death, one that he might, given his age, never see the end of. When I visited, I felt the huge, overpowering weight of this, something like grief, perhaps. Despite my own recovery, my knowledge of the condition did not help. I was aware of the low rate of remission, the absence of effective treatment, the possibility of further deterioration. I had long ago stopped thinking of myself as someone with chronic fatigue but the imprint was deep. I could not help identifying with my father, I could not separate myself from him. And when in 2008, three years into his own illness, I also began to unravel, it was this desperate existence which gradually came to feel like a vision of my own future.

PART TWO

Ghosthunting

I

MILE END ROAD LEADS NORTH OUT OF COLCHESTER, away from the railway station towards the A12, which shoots off towards Suffolk in one direction and Chelmsford and London in the other. It is a nondescript, rather windswept mishmash of Victorian and post-war housing, some uninviting pubs, a vet surgery, a closed-down beauty parlour. The arse end of the town, or one of them, anyway. It seemed to go on for ever, much further than I had imagined. I had never done the walk before, only looked at it on the map, but it had seemed like an important part of the process, measuring the distance. Now I regretted not getting the bus. After thirty minutes or so, however, I turned a corner and the view opened abruptly onto a system of broadly curving, freshly tarmacked roads; empty, traffic-lighted junctions; and roundabouts with high, clean, grey kerbs and muddy, freshly dug islands. I crossed towards the hospital site.

The visit to Severalls with my parents had set something going. My mother loaned me *Madness in its Place*, Diana Gittins' social history of the hospital, and as the months passed I began to wonder if I might write something myself. I had read that people with a legitimate interest – a local historian, two student documentary makers – had been allowed inside the old buildings, and so I enquired about access to the site. I was too late. Earlier in the year, a consortium of developers had been granted final approval to build 1,000 new homes. One of the developers replied to my email to say that the hospital was 'now undergoing a staged demolition and asbestos clearance' and as such was out of bounds to all visitors. This was a disappointment but I decided to go anyway. It was only now, several weeks later, as I approached on foot from the station, checking my progress on Google Maps, that I wondered really what I was doing there. I had not told anyone I was going – not Ellie or my parents – for fear of seeming ridiculous and because of an inability to explain what exactly I had in mind.

Things had changed significantly in the year since I had visited and the effect was disorientating. I could not tell which direction I had approached from with my parents or where we had parked up and looked over into the site. Beyond a high, spiked metal fence I counted five diggers working amongst deep trenches and the mounds of earth extracted from them. Teams of people in orange hard hats, high-vis jackets and clipboards consulted each other and directed the diggers. Large blue shipping containers, site offices or storage facilities, were dotted about. Huge pipes – part of a sewer system, I guessed – stuck out of the earth and more were being moved into position. Closer, on my side of the fence, there was a wide, freshly turfed, rising verge, newly planted at regular intervals with elm saplings, the beginning of some leafy new barricade, perhaps following the same outline as the fence and ditch that had once encircled the hospital site. Scattered more irregularly along the verge were clumps of daffodils, just beginning to bloom.

I continued along Via Urbis Romanae – an old name for a new road; Colchester peddles hard on its Roman origins – which skirts around the site and eventually links up with the A12. Along the fence the security notices were a constant: 'Danger: Demolition in Progress'; 'These Premises Are Patrolled by TCS (Total Care Security)'; 'Danger: Asbestos in This Area'; 'Guard Dogs on Site', alongside a black graphic of a dog's head, open-mouthed. Behind these warnings, past where the diggers and workmen had begun remaking the landscape, I could see some of the remaining hospital buildings, those scheduled for a later stage of the demolition presumably, or, in some cases, I had read, due to be retained. Around the buildings the earth was churned up into mud. Vehicle tracks criss-crossed the site in every direction. There were great pools of muddy water and stacks of metal fencing waiting to be erected.

A little further along the perimeter fence, I came to the sales office of one of the developers, a prefab box positioned on a corner, next to a site entrance busy with trucks and vans. To one side of the office, a huge banner hung from the fence. 'Welcome to Kingswood Heath,' it said – a name that skipped over recent history and dated back to the medieval period – 'a stunning collection of 1, 2, 3 and 4 bedroom homes set in an exceptional parkland environment, just minutes from the centre of Colchester'. Below this, several times actual size, was a picture of a quaintly – almost sinisterly – idealised family unit: mother and father, two blonde-haired children, a girl and a boy, all dressed in weekend outdoor gear, walking hand in hand down a sun-dappled country lane. The father points to something in the distance, out of view, and the eyes of the rest of the family are turned towards it.

The developer's brochure, which I had already received in the post, went into more detail. It described the opportunity for 'contemporary spacious living' amid 'green open spaces and mature wooded areas'. In addition to the homes a 'state of the art' gym and leisure centre with indoor and outdoor pools was already on site, as well as the brand new primary school, waiting to fill up with children from these as yet unbuilt estates. 'The new homes have been designed to sit in harmony with the traditional character of the development,' the brochure read, 'such as the historic water tower and original buildings which will be tastefully restored'. It evaded mention of what that 'traditional character' was or what 'the original buildings' were used for. And there was no mention of the name Severalls, or the Second Essex County Lunatic Asylum, but this seemed hardly surprising.

From the age of eleven to sixteen I went to school near Severalls. The school was new, built mainly to serve Highwoods, a housing development that was growing up gradually in the fields around it, and the kids from my village were bussed in and out every day to fill it in the meantime. The bus did not pass Severalls but we were all aware of it. Our orbit around school was small – at lunchtimes we walked to the huge new Tesco to buy lunch and sometimes we ran cross-country in the woods – but we knew the hospital was somewhere close, always out of view.

Already, in the mid- to late 1980s, Severalls was well past its prime, but it carried a potent mythology all the same and we were highly susceptible: a place where the strange, the deranged, and even the dangerous were kept in isolation from the rest of us. There were always rumours: older kids had gone over the perimeter fence at night and broken into the buildings; a maniac had escaped and was roaming the area. It was part of the everyday threat and abuse of school – that you would be sent there, that you belonged there – made almost banal by overuse. Severalls: the name alone carried a powerful taint of fear and shame. It spoke, I suppose, to the fear and mystery of mental illness, our undeveloped but intuitive sense of what it would mean to be cast out of normal society. Fear of the other, fear of the other within ourselves.

Thirty years later, as I had planned my trip – and even though I had already seen the ruins for myself when I went with my parents – I still felt this power, and when I searched for the hospital on the map I half expected not to find it there, an institutional or state secret, carefully erased from the records. It was there of course, 'Severalls Psychiatric Hospital', with its new status – 'Closed'. I saw, too, that it was even closer to my school than I had realised, just over a mile on foot. I flicked to Google Earth for satellite images and could see how much had already been demolished. A box came up on the right-hand side of the screen; the hospital had been awarded one star on the basis of a single Google Review. The review, in its entirety, read 'The torture was too much for me', and this had been liked three times.

I walked on past the banner advertising the new development and past the new primary school. I cut left down a bridleway that I had seen from the brochure or online was due to be turned into a cycle path that looped the entire development. I was now on a woodier track, rough and overgrown with trees and bushes, that continued to hug the perimeter of the development, not unlike the one pictured on the developer's banner, except for the high fence covered in orange plastic mesh that ran down one side. I had come, it seemed, to a quieter part of the site. Through the mesh I could see the same vehicle tracks and muddy pools and piles of unerected fencing, but no diggers or people at work. There were more buildings, a little closer to me now – again functional, unattractive, no doubt due for demolition. On the fence the same warnings continued: 'Danger: Keep Out'; 'Danger: Demolition in Progress'; 'Patrolled by Dogs'.

Weeks before, with the news that I would not be able to enter the site in any officially sanctioned way and the accounts of the urban explorers in my mind, I had considered a guerrilla mission of my own, perhaps enlisting the help of a bolder, savvier friend and the expertise of the people I had found online. This fantasy did not last long. I tried to picture myself kitted out in black, perhaps even with a balaclava, a flashlight and a camera – night-time entry seemingly the only viable option now that the development was in full swing – struggling over the fence or cutting my way through it. I had read a recent story in the local paper about a man who was taken to Accident and Emergency to have his finger sewn back on after slicing it off on the fence. I knew I could not manage it. Once, as a student, I went out spray painting with a friend, to act as lookout and assistant. I panicked at the first opportunity and somehow pulled the nozzle off one of his cans so that it was unusable, and he had looked at me in disgust. Now, jumpy and self-conscious simply walking the perimeter of the hospital site in the dull April light, my fantasy of a covert entry was even harder to imagine.

A little further on, however, the fence abruptly stopped, giving way to a vehicle track that went into the site and then disappeared around the buildings. There was no one around and no signs forbidding entry. It seemed like an oversight, an opportunity. I might plausibly pretend – to myself as much as anybody else – that I had wandered in unaware of any violation. The invitation was too much and so, adrenalin spiking, I went in.

I did not get far. A man in a high-vis jacket and hard hat hurried out of one of the buildings towards me, waving his arms.

'No. No entry,' he called out.

'I'm sorry,' I said, 'I didn't realise.'

'It's not safe.' His manner was wary rather than aggressive, as if unconvinced of his own authority, or as if I had caught him out, rather than the other way around.

'I was just looking around,' I said. 'I used to live near here.' This was not true, or at least quite a stretch.

This did not seem to clarify things and I thought then of something I had read, about inpatients of the old psychiatric hospitals who had been turned out into the community years before but still periodically returned, bewildered to find these places so changed, still expecting to be admitted. In Barbara Taylor's book *The Last Asylum*, she notes that this phenomenon was so common at Friern Hospital in north London that residents and security guards of the now redeveloped buildings were briefed about where to redirect them. Perhaps the man thought I was one of these, although I was hardly old enough, or, I thought, bewildered enough.

'Are you knocking everything down?' I asked. I knew the answer to this but the question seemed to relax him a little and we began to walk back towards the gap in the fence.

He shrugged. 'Some,' he said. 'I'm not sure.'

I nodded and stepped back onto the path. Careful not to turn and look back, I continued to follow the fence on the other side, the adrenalin rush beginning to drain away.

I walked quickly on. I wondered if any kind of alert had gone out, that someone had been caught wandering around the site with unclear – perhaps nefarious – intentions. I needn't have worried. I saw no one else at close range and had no further encounters. As I reached the north-west corner of the site, the furthest point from where I had started, the landscape on the other side of the fence began to change. Stands of tall pines and grassland appeared, something closer to the rolling gardens and lawns for which Severalls was known and to the 'green open spaces and mature wooded areas' trumpeted in the developer's brochure.

I could see, from a raised bank and through the fence, the front of the main hospital building, the so-called Administration Building. It stood at the head of a circular drive, once the point of entry and departure for patients, staff and visitors, the portal to the enclosed world of the institution. Two storeys high, red brick, crowned with elaborate stone cornicing, a clock tower mounted centrally on the roof, it was just about possible to imagine how elegant and imposing it must have seemed. Now, however, with its windows boarded up, the brickwork blackened with dirt, the clock face cracked, and piles of smashed-up wood and mangled metal sitting outside, presumably the building's gutted interior, it was utterly diminished.

I had nearly finished a circuit of the perimeter when I passed a modern, one-storey, flat-roofed building that sat outside the fenced-off area of the site. The car park was busy with people arriving and leaving. This was the St Aubyn Centre, an NHS adolescent acute and intensive care unit for young people with serious mental health problems – the only one in the south of England, I discovered when I looked it up later, and by this time the only remaining mental health service on the Severalls site. The centre has two wards, one of which is Longview Ward. There is a small school on the site, also known as Longview, and I remembered the name. When I was eleven or twelve my friend Stephen had started refusing to go to school. He was, as far as anyone else could see, a straightforward kid, well liked and easy-going, and it didn't seem to make any sense. Eventually he was sent to Longview, a place that carried a similar aura of mystery and dread to Severalls, a place for the most troubled, the most difficult kids, although Stephen was not like that. We had seen each other nearly every day for a couple of years, riding our bikes around the village in the afternoons and at weekends, but he never came back to our school and I lost track of him after that. Years later, I heard that he had gone to college and then opened a bar in Colchester – I guessed that meant he was doing OK – but though I thought of him from time to time we were never in touch again.

2

ATIVAN IS A BRAND NAME FOR LORAZEPAM, A BENZO-
diazepine that was first brought to market by the US
pharmaceutical company Wyeth in 1977 as a treatment for
short-term anxiety, insomnia and acute seizures and for the
sedation of aggressive hospital patients. It is regarded as
more powerful and longer-acting than most other benzodiazepines, such as Valium, with comparably greater potential
for dependency and addiction. An early advertisement to
potential consumers in the US shows a rising sun burst-
ing out from behind a vast and shadowy mountain, its rays
fanning out over the dark terrain, a sort of Blakean vision
of enlightenment or paradise found. 'Now it can be yours,'
it reads, 'The Ativan Experience'. Another ad, from 1987,
when the risks of benzodiazepine use had become more
widely known, opts for the same kind of sublime imagery,
although this time the vision seems a little more tentative,
existential: a blue and green Earth suspended in black space,
the sun reduced to a pale glow behind the top right side of
the globe. 'In a world where certainties are few...' it reads,

'no wonder Ativan is prescribed by so many caring clinicians'. Despite its hubris, the first ad, the blazing sun bearing down on the shrouded valley, is the kind of metaphor I might have come up with myself if I'd had to describe my experience – rising from my bed, physical symptoms vanished, appetite returned and mind cleared – of taking the drug for the first time.

In contrast, the citalopram was not working. After four weeks, I went back to the GP. Although I had not planned to, and Chris had made me promise not to, I told the doctor that I had been taking Ativan. I told her how well it worked and asked if she could prescribe it to me. She frowned. 'I've worked a lot in this area,' she said, 'and we only give that type of drug to people who are terminally ill in hospital. They make you feel good because they are very strong. I don't recommend it at all.'

She wrote me a prescription for another week of sleeping tablets and doubled my dose of citalopram, from twenty to forty milligrams per day. 'Sometimes it needs that much,' she told me. 'Give it another few weeks.' With the doctor's warning in mind, I tried to take the Ativan less often. Sometimes I took just half a pill, and the effect was barely noticeable. I had terrible days. I clung to the hope that the increased dose of citalopram would make a difference but hardly believed it. I read more online. Citalopram was not an anti-anxiety drug as such. It was a selective serotonin reuptake inhibitor or SSRI, like Prozac, that had been found to have anxiety-reducing properties for a high percentage of people who took it.

Anxiety and depression are very often diagnosed together, 'comorbid' is the term, and this seemed logical to me – they might have similar causes, and one might feed into the other. I recognised some elements of depression in how I was feeling but I felt strongly that this was not the right term for what was happening to me. People with depression usually described an absence of feeling, a numbness. If anything, I was experiencing an overabundance of feeling. Everything was heightened, excruciatingly so: I was over-stimulated to the point of paralysis. Also, I had an objective sense that my life was good, if only I could solve the problem of this anxiety. I saw it as something distinct from me, something other, something attacking me, an invader. I did not hate myself, I hated how I was feeling, and this distinction seemed significant. I was not preoccupied with hurting myself. And where depression usually seemed to be discreet, shameful, a private torture, my anxiety was florid, public. I talked about it to anyone who would listen.

After a further three weeks on citalopram I went back to the doctor again. I asked her if it ever took that long to start working. 'It can,' she said, but she didn't sound convinced. She said we could try another SSRI, but I could not face the prospect of withdrawing from one drug – I had read many terrifying stories about this online – and beginning on another. The doctor nodded. 'In reality,' she said, 'there isn't much difference between them. It's mainly branding.'

I had been in touch with a friend of a friend in the US, a psychiatrist. 'This problem,' he wrote of my anxiety, 'is usually to do with a biologic predisposition, genetically determined. The most common mistake made by health providers is under-treating. The most effective treatment requires the use of a number of medications: polypharmacy.' He mentioned a number of drugs and told me to discuss them with my doctor. The GP shook her head. None were appropriate, she said, and some weren't even available here. She wasn't unsympathetic. She said she would refer me to the counselling service they ran at the surgery. I started to cry and she told me to just keep going, things would get better. I didn't mention the Ativan and she didn't ask.

I left the surgery in despair. As far as I could tell, the doctor had run out of ideas; there was nothing more she could do for me. At times, usually in the evenings, when the anxiety tended naturally to abate, it was possible to rational-ise it all, an understandable – and therefore likely temporary – reaction to particular circumstances and stresses. And yet whilst it seemed impossible that the anxiety could continue at this intensity and not somehow burn itself out, everything I read online said that it was a chronic condition, manage-able perhaps, but not curable. I had changed and would never be quite the same. The switch had been flipped and could not be flipped back.

I tried to understand what had happened to me. My life seemed, suddenly and profoundly, to have split into two parts, a before and an after. The person who had managed to get to this point in life – to go to school and university, to work, to travel, to make friends, to find places to live, to have a relationship and a child – was unrecognisable. I thought often about a recurring dream I had as a child, a generic sort of nightmare, which seemed now to have the blunt symbolism of a premonition. In the dream I was walking alone up the side of a grassy hill amongst trees and flowers in bright sunshine, happy and hopeful of what I would find on the other side. But each time I crested the hill I would begin to sense something ahead of me, something formless and intangible, but utterly terrifying. The feeling grew and grew but I was powerless to stop walking towards it, until the dream ended in a crescendo of terror.

However, the Ativan had demonstrated something important to me. The belief that I was relapsing into chronic fatigue, the far more debilitating version of it that had left my father housebound, had been the dominant thread of my anxiety in the early weeks of becoming ill, perhaps even the precipitator of it. But the Ativan had made it clear that my physical symptoms were the result of anxiety itself – not some other illness, not some tricky virus – and this was a form of complicated relief. Until this crisis, I had thought about my health as a struggle against the weakness, fallibility and inadequacy of my physical self. Now I found myself forced to reconsider, to accept the possibility that the vulnerability was a mental one, that this was at the root of everything. In this interpretation, the nerve doctors of the 19th century had diagnosed me correctly after all – a neurotic, a neurasthenic, a hysteric.

What was happening to me now was undoubtedly different in degree from my previous malaise, a major escalation. I had never before had the sense that my mind was unmanageable, out of control, a splitting of my mental self. But this did not mean that it had not been working to undermine me in more subtle, unreadable ways for years. Perhaps my life was not split into two parts after all. And, in fact, if I was tempted to build a narrative, to join the dots – and I was – it was possible to go even further back, to the persistent fevers and exhaustion of my A levels, and before that, the vicious, blinding migraines between the ages of twelve and fourteen. It was therefore not true to say that my mental health had been uneventful – it had simply been misunderstood, misidentified. I had always been faulty, some flaw or uneasiness in the blood that was sometimes dormant, then morphing and mutating.

I filled notebooks with scrawled, near-illegible notes that tried to rationalise it all away. Mantras like 'it's only anxiety' or 'this too shall pass', something my father had said to me on the phone, copied out day after day, and lists of people whose situation seemed worse than my own: the friend of a friend, the same age as me, who had been paralysed by a catastrophic stroke; the friend whose girlfriend had been killed in a car crash; broadening out and out to the homeless, refugees fleeing their homes, people whose children had died. In other lists I wrote down all the good things I had – Ellie, my daughter, the rest of my family, a home, a job, a book that was being published.

Mostly, though, it was not open to rationalisation, and my grim perspective saturated the wider world, too. I was excruciatingly sensitive to the pain and suffering that I saw everywhere. I couldn't watch television. The soaps were full of misery cranked up to the maximum. The relentless and hollow cheeriness of children's television presenters was an expression of the futility of everything. The news was out of the question. Only the blandest feel-good radio was manageable. The exception was a ghoulish and obsessive interest in the personal traumas of celebrities, their addictions, breakdowns and overdoses; I felt a special connection to them. When I was driven – I was in no state to drive myself – down streets of houses belonging to people I did not know and had never seen, I felt the weight of all their sadness and difficulties, their tragic fences and pitiful garages.

The house we had bought was still being redecorated, and as well as looking after me and our daughter and going to work, on most days Ellie went to speak to the builders. I was contributing nothing. I could not work or make decisions about the house or look after our child. Instead, I had turned myself into an added burden – a self-pitying, incapable burden – and the awareness of this only compounded my anxiety. On better days I went with Ellie to the house. It was on a private estate of identical houses built in the 1960s, set in a pristine landscape of communal lawns and woodland, but the house itself was being dismembered. Collapsing ceilings were being replaced, internal walls knocked down and the entire rotted front of the house rebuilt. I stood there uselessly amongst the debris, eating the bits of banana and dark chocolate that were sustaining me, and it was hard not to see this chaos as a metaphor for my own disarray. This unfamiliar house, in a part of London that I did not know, seemed to bring the sense of alienation from my old life, my old self, into even starker relief.

I thought more about my parents. I had identified strongly with my father's chronic fatigue but I knew he had been ill before that. I saw now that the patterns might go further back, patterns that fitted this different model of illness, a model that was more psychological than physical – the genetic predisposition that the psychiatrist in the US whom I had been in touch with had insisted upon. 'It breaks my heart to see you like this,' my mother said one day when she was visiting me, and I felt she was acknowledging something more than my own present wretchedness. I had not dodged the bullet after all. It had been there all along, lodged inside me.

3

ON THE MORNING OF HIS ADMISSION TO SEVERALLS in June 1968 my father remembers sitting in a wheelchair at one end of the main corridor, once the longest in Europe, a corridor so long that he could not see where it ended. He was taken to a ward and later he sat in a consulting room, now in a dressing gown, in front of a horseshoe of eight or nine people discussing his condition. He was in tears but also relieved because finally there was an acknowledgement that something was wrong with him. After a while his psychiatrist, Dr Fox, said, 'I think we'll go for modified insulin therapy.'

My father was in a ward with twelve other patients, some of whom were receiving the same treatment. Every morning, those who were not on modified insulin therapy all went to breakfast. The others remained on the ward and at 8 a.m. Nurse Beaney came around with a medical trolley, drew the curtains around the beds and gave each of the patients an injection of insulin. Every half hour he came back to take their pulse and temperature, until 11.30 a.m.

when their breakfast was brought in. By this time, my father and his fellow patients, tanked up with insulin, were ravenous. They ate a large breakfast and when lunch was brought in at twelve they ate that, too.

Insulin helps the body move blood sugar into the cells. People with type 1 diabetes inject it in order to reduce the level of sugar in the blood and avoid the symptoms of hyperglycaemia. An excess of insulin causes the cells to absorb too much sugar, risking a hypoglycaemic reaction instead. In a mild case, the symptoms of a hypo range from sweating and light-headedness to anxiety and a rapid heartbeat. Severe hypoglycaemia can lead to seizures, unconsciousness and death. The original application of insulin in psychiatry was called insulin shock therapy. It induced a temporary coma and was used mainly as a treatment for patients with schizophrenia. Nobel Prize winning mathematician John Nash received the treatment for his paranoid schizophrenia. In *A Beautiful Mind*, the film of Nash's life, Russell Crowe is strapped to the hospital bed and receives the injection in his arm. A tear wells from his eye before he falls unconscious. Then, as the music swells, two bits are placed in his mouth to stop him biting off his tongue, and he starts to convulse violently, his wrists and arms straining at their bindings, his eyes closed throughout. (Crowe was nominated for an Oscar but didn't win.)

Insulin shock therapy had been phased out by the time my father was in Severalls. In the modified version, developed in the 1930s as a treatment for neurosis, patients were given an increased dose until the insulin flooding the system caused 'a reaction', as Dr Fox described it to my father. The principle was not dissimilar to electroconvulsive therapy or ECT, then known as electroshock therapy, which a number of patients on my father's ward were receiving: that a physical shock to the system, such as a seizure, could bring about abrupt remission from psychological symptoms, a kind of reset, the exact mechanism of which was mysterious.

'What is a reaction?' my father asked.

Dr Fox told him, 'You'll know when you have one.'

My father was twenty-eight years old. He and my mother had been married for two years, and he had just finished his second year as a mathematics lecturer at Essex University. The university itself was new, part of a wave of higher-education expansion that had left him with seven different job offers around the country. He does not remember now why he chose Essex. The sprawling main building, a series of descending squares with fountains in the middle, was still under construction when my father visited for interview. Modelled on the plan of a Tuscan hill village but reimagined as modernist brutalism, it was an experiment that never quite worked; a concrete spaceship crashed into a shallow Essex valley. The North Sea winds rushed around the raised concrete walkways, tunnels and squares and created unpredictable vortexes of air that could knock you off your feet. Aesthetics dictated that the buildings were designed without windowsills and so the rain ran directly down the walls, staining the concrete. Students were accommodated in tower blocks, although only six of the twenty-eight planned towers were ever built. I remember hearing that this was because in the early years too many students committed suicide by jumping out of them, but this could well be apocryphal. Still, the university shared the high idealism of the times. Its goal, the founding Vice Chancellor Albert Sloman said in the Reith Lectures of 1963, was 'to emphasise the fundamental unity of human knowledge' and provide 'a truly liberal education'. My father was idealistic, too. He was committed to teaching and determined to make a good job of it.

My mother also worked at the university in the registrar's office, and they had moved into an old chauffeur's cottage in Dedham, a famously pretty village on the border with Suffolk. On the final day of exams at the end of their first year there, the summer of 1967, my parents had arranged to meet friends to play tennis when my father collapsed suddenly with chest pains. My mother drove him to the doctor's surgery and said she thought he was having a heart attack. The doctor dismissed this and sent my father home with pills – amphetamines, he later discovered – that kept him up all night, his heart beating furiously. On the way back to the doctor's the following morning his legs buckled under him, and the man from the local garage drove him home. He spent the next three months in bed, trying but failing to go to work. In October, when teaching began again, he went to see the head of department. 'You need to get back on the job,' he told my father, and marched him straight round to a lecture theatre.

My father set up a camp bed in his office and for the rest of the year he lay there whenever he was not required to deliver a lecture or a tutorial or be at a meeting. By March 1968 the student protests had begun at universities in Europe and the US. At Essex three students gatecrashed a lecture by Dr Thomas Inch, a scientist at the Atomic Weapons Research Establishment at Aldermaston, and covered him with flour. When the university suspended them, students burnt cars in the main square, occupied the campus and declared it a 'Free University'. My father, like many of the other young, left-wing academics, was sympathetic to the students, but he did not feel well enough to get involved. He remembers lying on his camp bed, the smell of smoke coming through the window. He had grown a beard. Dr Fox, to whom he had been referred by his GP for treatment as an outpatient, remarked, 'Asserting your masculinity, are you?'

My parents were due to move house but when he woke up on the morning of the move my father was in a state of high anxiety, unable to get out of bed. My mother phoned Dr Fox and he arranged for my father to be admitted to Severalls.

By the time my father went to Severalls in 1968, it was a very different institution from the one that had been opened to great fanfare in 1913. In fact, the asylum at Colchester had only been established for seventeen years before it was rebranded. Even in this short period much had changed in the hospital psychiatric system and much had been done to try to throw off the stigma of the old asylums. In 1930 the Mental Treatment Act ended the official use of the term 'asylum' altogether, lunatics became patients, and voluntary patients were admitted for the first time. The Second Essex County Lunatic Asylum became the Essex and Colchester Mental Hospital, Severalls. Some residents were allowed 'grand parade', meaning they were free to roam the immediate countryside, the permitted range marked by signs on the roads that read 'No Severalls Patients Beyond This Point'. Some took advantage of this new freedom to run away. Before 1959 it was hard to be decertified – once you were insane, you stayed insane – but a loophole meant that a patient who absconded and was not caught within fourteen days became legally free, a practice known, wonderfully, as 'wandering away'. Between 1913 and 1937, 245 patients at Severalls wandered away. One of these patients sent a postcard, another posted back his hospital clothes.

As well as a change in the culture, there was hope for new treatments, too. Desperate for the kind of radical advances that had been seen in general medicine, and the status and recognition they would bring the profession, many psychiatrists pursued innovative treatments that seemed to offer rapid biomedical fixes to mental problems. Severalls was no exception to this development. Beginning in the 1930s, sleep therapy or 'prolonged narcosis' was used at the hospital to treat psychosis and neurosis. Injections of barbiturates or opiates kept patients asleep for up to a month, an extreme version of the rest cure that was said to leave sufferers rejuvenated and symptom-free upon waking. Between injections patients became conscious enough to be fed, washed and changed, before receiving another dose. A programme of prolonged baths – hours or days at a time in lukewarm water – was also popular with Severalls doctors, and new bathing facilities had to be built to accommodate the demand. In 1928 an old waiting room was converted into a pathology lab. The pathologist performed post-mortems on patients' bodies as well as injected rabbits and guinea pigs with extracts from patients' sputum and faeces in an effort to diagnose what they had been suffering from. In 1951, Cyril Bush Taylor, a technician in the lab, collapsed after catching an infection from one of the specimens he was examining. He was treated at the National Hospital for Nervous Diseases in London and then, in a twist that seems almost too neat to be true, returned to Severalls as a patient.

Insulin shock therapy and ECT were adopted at Severalls after the war. The latter had been developed in part from the observation that people with epilepsy, who suffered seizures as a matter of course, seemed to be immune from depression. Sometimes the two treatments were combined and patients were given ECT when they were in an insulin-induced coma. At first Severalls had difficulties administering ECT because its own electricity supply was not compatible with the new machines, but convertors were bought and it soon became the preferred treatment for schizophrenia and severe depression. One nurse at the Severalls ECT unit in the 1950s described how, at that time, 'There was no anaesthesia – oh no, no, no. It was just sort of rough the way we did it then. They'd lay down, you used to give the injection – a muscle relaxant – 'cause, you see, once they got it on, some of these doctors were cruel. They used to go, "I'll give him one for luck!" Hold 'em down, you have to hold 'em down... Some of the young doctors, they used to love to do it.'

In 1951, Mr Sherwood, a surgeon at the London Hospital, began to carry out lobotomies at Severalls. Two years earlier Portuguese neurologist António Egas Moniz had received the Nobel Prize for developing this pioneering treatment – also known as leucotomy – which claimed to be able to cure various forms of mental illness by drilling holes into the skull and destroying the frontal lobes of the brain. The practice took off. In the early 1950s an American evangelist for the procedure, Walter Freeman, a neurologist with no surgical training, developed a simplified, efficient technique for carrying out a lobotomy: an ice pick driven under the eyelid with blunt force. He delivered this himself in the back of his self-styled 'lobotomobile', a van he drove around the mental hospitals of North America, for $25 per patient. Pictures show the goateed Freeman leaning out of the cab of the lobotomobile, waving extravagantly, like one of the Merry Pranksters.

Mr Sherwood was less of a showman, but his work was, at first, highly praised. By 1956, he had operated on 308 patients at Severalls. A nurse described the miraculous recovery of one patient: 'He was a well-educated man, very depressed, and they gave him a course of ECT and everything, and it didn't help him at all. So they gave him a leucotomy. And within six months he was one of the air controllers at London Airport.' But not everyone benefited. Other patients' mental faculties were destroyed, one caught an infection and another committed suicide, and it became apparent that Sherwood was carrying out his own unapproved experiments, injecting different substances into patients' brains to see how they would react. One nurse recalled, 'Sherwood said, "well I'm going to put this thing in, you know." Well, it's not that I'm frightened of needles – but this wasn't just a needle! I mean it was something – God knows what he was doing!' Eventually the *News of the World* got hold of the story, questions were asked in parliament and Sherwood's contract was cancelled.

Until the 1950s many patients were heavily drugged with paraldehyde and the wards stank of its unpleasant, vinegary odour. In 1951, with the development of chlorpromazine, a modified antihistamine, many psychiatrists believed they had found the miracle drug that would be as significant for the treatment of mental illness as the discovery of penicillin had become for physical illness less than a decade earlier. Marketed in the UK as Largactil (a compression of 'large action'), it was the first of the so-called antipsychotics and under its influence formerly violent, disturbed and disruptive patients became calm, passive, manageable. In 1954 Largactil started to be used in Severalls but was quickly suspended when a number of patients died from receiving massive doses – five in one night according to some sources. In 1957 it was reintroduced with tighter controls over dosage and became a standard treatment, changing life on the wards dramatically. Previously psychotic or chronic patients were better able to function, engaging in other therapies and sometimes taking on jobs in the hospital or its gardens.

However, the side effects were numerous. In her memoir *Giving Up the Ghost*, Hilary Mantel described taking Largactil: 'It was not a friendly drug; it made my throat jump and close, as if someone were hanging me. This is how a mad person appears to the world – lips trembling, speech fumbling and jerky.' Eventually, though not before chlorpromazine had been prescribed to fifty million people worldwide, the symptoms Mantel and others described were linked to tardive dyskinesia, an incurable neurological condition caused by the drug. A nurse at Severalls described how the Largactil syrup tasted 'like a good Bristol Cream Sherry'. At Christmas parties staff used it as a cocktail ingredient. A deputy matron who was particularly partial to the taste – and presumably the effect – was found one morning passed out on the cricket pitch.

4

MENTAL ILLNESS HAS BEEN DESCRIBED AS A WAR OF self versus self and this was how it felt to me. When I took an Ativan, for the six or seven hours that followed, this war abated, was put on hold; more than this, it showed me that in the absence of the war, my old, my recognisable self – my true self, I felt – was still there and intact.

We had moved out of the flat and into the new house, but I felt no better. Without the hope of some other resolution to the problem, I began to take the Ativan more often. When the sleeping pills the doctor had given me ran out, I began to take Ativan at night, too. Supplies arrived every week or so from Chris and on the appointed day I waited anxiously for the post to arrive. The foil strip of ten pills was wrapped in a tissue, designed, I suppose, to disguise what was inside the envelope or perhaps to stop the sharp edges of the foil tearing the paper. Stuck to the tissue was a Post-it note, always with the same message: 'As promised – try and make these ones last!'

I did try. I obsessed over each one, weighing short-term

relief against the dangers of addiction. I reminded myself that, even now, the quantities I was taking were very small, no more than a single one-milligram pill at a time, and there were days when I forced myself not to take one at all. I reminded myself that I had never been addicted to any other drugs or to alcohol. In fact, even before this crisis, I barely drank and had not so much as smoked a joint for nearly ten years. I pointed out to myself that I was not taking them for fun or to get high, but out of a kind of necessity, in order to feel normal.

But perhaps this was an exact definition of addiction – taking something to feel normal – and I read the online testimonies of people whose problems had escalated from just such a minimal, temporary benzodiazepine habit as this. People with wives and husbands and kids and jobs and mortgages. I read about how quickly your tolerance developed so that you had to take more to get the same effect. How the more you took, the more fiercely the anxiety responded, a monster that only became hungrier the more you fed it. All this made sense to the puritan in me. You could not take something that made you feel so much better without paying some kind of price. How could you not become addicted to feeling this much better? I remembered the doctor's words at my second appointment. That these days they only gave benzodiazepines to the terminally ill – as pain relief? To take away the fear of death? – presumably because they wouldn't have to live with the consequences of being hooked. I knew this couldn't quite be true. After all, Chris's GP was still prescribing Ativan to him. But I could see that this was different. He was older than me and had been on it for years; perhaps his doctor saw little benefit in trying to get him off it now.

Taking benzodiazepines could only go one way, it seemed – a grimly tightening spiral that led to long-term dependency and addiction, ever-increasing anxiety and depression, or, if you tried to cut down or stopped taking them altogether, the hallucinations, seizures and psychosis of withdrawal. It was striking how often Ativan, amongst the many available benzodiazepines, came up in these horror stories. Valium, it seemed, was often used to wean people off its more dangerous sister drug. Perhaps I was not yet physically hooked but the psychological dependency seemed clear enough: the way I fretted when my supply ran low and counted out the days I could make them last, the relief when the envelope from Chris dropped onto the doormat. And it was true that the days off between the pills were becoming fewer.

Then there was the nature of my supply. It would be one thing to be using a drug like this when the doctor was giving it to me, for it to be part of an approved clinical treatment, but it was another to be taking it illicitly, to be making my own amateur judgements about what was safe and sensible. This felt like even more dangerous terrain, the preserve of junkies and crackheads using it to take the edge off their other addictions – 'blues', 'downers', 'blue heaven' were the street vernacular for Ativan, my online research told me. These possibilities weren't only in my head. I knew that Ellie was uneasy, disapproving, as were the few friends who knew what I was doing.

And anyway, how reliable was the supply from Chris? What if his own prescription was cut or stopped? He wasn't young and I found myself wondering – a sign of how narrow and obsessive my fears had become – what would happen if he died? I began to look into online suppliers, the possibility of buying illegally and in bulk from India.

When benzodiazepines arrived on the market in the 1960s, more effective and with significantly less risk of overdose than barbiturates, they quickly became a phenomenon, as significant a reference point for the historical moment as the contraceptive pill. From 1969 to 1982 Valium was the best-selling drug in the US, and this went hand in hand with a new democratisation of mental illness – at least in its milder forms – to an experience no longer confined to psychiatric hospitals but common to the general population. Questions of mental health and lifestyle were now blurred, at least by the pharmaceutical companies who stood to gain, and these drugs were marketed direct to the public – at least in the US – like any other consumer product: a washing machine, a car, a holiday.

But even before the risks of dependency and withdrawal became widely known, the drugs had an image problem, of sorts. The Rolling Stones nailed it as early as 1966 in 'Mother's Little Helper'. Loaded on heroin and cocaine, they patronised the suburban housewife who overdosed on tranquillizers because she could not cope with the trivial strains of cooking for her husband. Valium and its equiva-lents represented the *other* drug culture. Not the subversive, countercultural, technicolour, epiphanic visions of LSD and marijuana but the greyness, conformity, passivity, stultification and control of consumerism, the suburbs, the military–industrial complex and the Man. You dropped acid to become truly alive, to open the doors of perception and see the world as it really was or could be. You took a Valium to anaesthetise yourself against a reality you couldn't cope with.

There were ironies in all this for me. In my late teens and twenties I had wanted to try everything. For me and my friends, taking drugs was part of playing music, going out, having a good time, finding out who we were. I had wanted to run these risks – insofar as there were risks – and it was often fun, but I was never really a natural. Weed, at least the strong stuff, made me edgy and strung out. On the one occasion I ate some hash I lay on the pavement outside a pub and vomited for hours. Hallucinogens – acid or mushrooms – were too intense to be called enjoyable, and the comedowns were brutal. Cocaine didn't deliver the buzz it always seemed to promise and the sense of self-loathing that followed was never worth it. Only Ecstasy seemed like a straightforward pleasure and I came to it late, when my nervousness about my health had already begun to assert itself. In contrast, Ativan was a perfect fit. It was the thing – the only thing – I trusted at that time, the thing that made me feel good: *my drug*. It seemed I was now more suburban than subversive. And yet, taking this legally manufactured drug, developed to treat exactly the illness I was suffering from, felt like the most transgressive behaviour of my life.

I had been taking it for months now and the habit had taken on a different texture, both more prosaic and more covert. I kept one in my wallet at all times, pressed down into a corner behind my bank cards, and often checked for it with a finger, the hard, sharp edge of the foil-covered plastic. I no longer told Ellie every time I had taken one, though often I felt that she knew. When I was expecting an envelope from Chris I lurked around the front door at the time the postman was due then smuggled it upstairs to my desk drawer. I stopped mentioning Ativan to friends, who I felt would be alarmed to know I was still taking it. On occasions when I took one in a public place, on a train or in a supermarket, I turned against a wall or a window and fumbled over my wallet. The first thing I did when I got home was to replace it with another from the drawer.

After three months on sick leave, I went back to work. I disliked the job, in a university administration office, and had felt trapped in it for a long time, but the prospect of losing it was far worse. Work was hard, and sometimes horrible, but it was preferable to the churning worry of not being there. I was so anxious about not coping that, to my surprise, I found myself oddly efficient and conscientious, probably a better, more engaged employee than I had been before.

But, in front of a computer all day, I spent more and more time in the forums and chatrooms dedicated to anxiety and how to treat it. The internet might have been created for just this purpose – an anonymous, unregulated, limitless frontier for the troubled, frustrated, desperate legions to expand into. They were not out in the world, a world they could not cope with, but they were here, online. I gravitated to the sites that focused on benzodiazepines, looking, I suppose, for some defining piece of information that would finally reassure me or convince me to stop. I did not find it. I found other sufferers with usernames like *BenzoBoy* or *QueenOfPills* or *DrVacant* and an atmosphere concentrated with their misery, self-pity and anger. I minimised the windows whenever someone passed my desk and deleted my browsing history several times a day. I had told my close colleagues about the anxiety and the antidepressants, but the Ativan remained a secret.

Throughout this time, I carried on taking citalopram, not because I thought it had any positive effect, but because I was afraid of withdrawal symptoms if I stopped. I attended the course of counselling sessions at the doctor's surgery, where I was asked to rate my feelings on a scale of one to ten and set targets for things I felt I ought to do – drive the car, go out in the evening and see friends, or start writing again. When these sessions ended and I told the GP they had not helped, she referred me to a psychiatrist. It was nine months since the beginning of my breakdown.

The appointment was at a scruffy, anonymous-looking building on a south London high street. There was a series of security doors to be buzzed through, and inside the comfortless waiting room a receptionist sat behind a thick glass screen. I thought immediately – melodramatically – of the highly disturbed attacking people or having to be restrained. The psychiatrist, when I saw him, seemed worn out and disengaged, used to dealing with much more desperate cases than my own. He mentioned the names of some drugs that he could prescribe but without great conviction, and when I looked them up later they were all antipsychotics of the kind mainly given to people with schizophrenia. He gave me an appointment for three months' time but I did not go back.

A year after I became unwell my collection of short stories was published. When the first box of copies arrived I could not bear to look at them. Ellie had had the cover of the book blown up and framed as a surprise but I could not bear to look at this either, and instead of putting it on the wall, I gave it to my mother and father. I had worked on the book for nine years and fantasised about it for much longer. The thing I had wanted most had become a reality but I could take no pleasure in it. The gap between how I felt and how I knew I was supposed to feel was too great and too painful.

There were some good reviews, some mediocre reviews and a couple of bad ones. It was all the same to me. I went through the motions of promoting the book in a daze. I took part in events where I stood up in front of audiences and pretended to be the same person who had written the book and was thrilled to see it published, when in fact it was all just a reminder of how I would never be able to write again. One of the interviews that appeared began, 'Tom Lee must be a happy man…' and this seemed like a cruel joke. Sometimes, I wondered if it could be that after years of work, of hope and frustration, of maintaining the conviction that I could be a writer, of a gnawing fear of failure,

the reality of it had fundamentally weakened whatever structures I had built to preserve myself. Now that the dream was
at its most tangible it was slipping away from me.

When I went to events and read the stories themselves
out loud – grim, claustrophobic, paranoid stories – I suddenly saw what I had missed before, that here was an intimate
record of my own increasingly fraught mental state. Here
again was evidence of the years of anxiety that I had not
recognised at the time, or so it seemed to me now. Almost
every one of the stories ended – like my recurring childhood nightmare – on a cliffhanger of unresolved distress,
their characters apparently on the brink of psychic collapse.
I had anticipated myself. Quite often, to get through these
readings, I took a pill.

5

MY FATHER WAS AN INPATIENT AT SEVERALLS FOR six weeks. Each day he was injected with an increased dose of insulin. Then he lay there, his pulse and temperature taken every half hour, waiting for something to happen, 'the reaction' Dr Fox had alluded to. It is hard to see how this experience would have been good for his nerves.

My father recalls his time in hospital in detail – names, incidents, things that were said – heightened no doubt by the strangeness and intensity of the experience and memorialised by frequent retellings. In the bed by the entrance to the ward was Joe, an old man who never spoke but retched continually into a small pot. After lunch every day Joe went into the television room, where he spent all afternoon watching horse racing. One day, my father remembers, Joe's brother came to visit. Joe came alive. They talked animatedly for hours about the racing and trips to the Derby, and the pot was forgotten. When his brother went Joe was silent again, except for the sound of his retching. In the bed next to my father was a man named Cliff, who had a large glass bowl by the side of his bed that he urinated into. He was a heavy smoker and when he finished a cigarette he leaned over and dropped it into the bowl, where it fizzled out. Smoking at night was forbidden but Cliff did it anyway and by the time the nurse came in the morning to empty the bowl, it was swimming with piss-bloated butts. Cliff and my father got on well. He wrote poetry and carved things out of wood. He gave one of these to my father, which he kept and showed me fifty years later, a four-leaf clover the size of a bottle top.

My mother visited every day and got to know the staff and other patients. She had a gift for making friends, as my father once said to me. There was a putting green in the grounds and although my father was too exhausted to take part, on sunny days he sat and watched my mother go around the course. Another man my father liked, Bryan, said he was the heir to the Mister Softee ice cream empire. He said he had been arrested when he got off the boat from Holland at Harwich. The police had thrown a mattress on top of him and started jumping on it, before sectioning him. At Severalls, he played for the patients' cricket eleven. He got on well with my mother, too, and when he was discharged from Severalls but my father was still in hospital, he went to visit her at home in Dedham. She gave him dinner, lent him £10 and never saw him again.

Despite the arcane treatment my father was receiving, Severalls in 1968 was a more progressive institution than it had been even a few years before. By the end of the 1950s, the mood had moved against psychiatric hospitals, just as it had against the asylums. In 1961 Enoch Powell, the Minister of Health, announced the government's intention to close them. 'There they stand,' Powell told the National Association for Mental Health, 'isolated, majestic, imperious, brooded over by the gigantic water-tower... the asylums which our forefathers built with such immense solidity to express the notions of their day... For the great majority of these institutions there is no appropriate future use.'

In 1960 Severalls had appointed a new physician superintendent. Only thirty-seven years old, Russell Barton was a bold and energetic psychiatric reformer, a maverick and a thinker, of a kind who had turned up frequently before in the history of mental health care. Early in his career Barton had ECT administered to himself to determine what it was like for patients. Based on this experience, he insisted that the treatment never be given without an anaesthetic. In 1959 he published *Institutional Neurosis*, a slim but excoriating critique of the psychiatric hospital system written whilst he was working at Shenley Hospital in Hertfordshire. In it he argued that patients became so institutionalised that this itself constituted a further form of mental illness. Barton described the symptoms, some of them easily observable. 'The patient often adopts a characteristic posture, the hands held across the body or tucked behind an apron, the shoulders drooped and the head held forward. The gait has a shuffling quality, movements at the pelvis, hips and knees are restricted, although physical examination shows a full range of movement at these joints.'

Institutional Neurosis anticipated much of the so-called anti-psychiatry movement of the 1960s. In 1961 Erving Goffman's *Asylums* described the regime at a 7,000-patient psychiatric hospital in Washington DC and concluded that it did nothing to help patients or restore them to health but instead was organised only to coerce them into playing a role. In the same year Thomas Szasz argued in *The Myth of Madness* that mental illness was a construct, a tool that was used to deal with those whom society deemed unacceptable. Michel Foucault in France, Franco Basaglia in Italy and R. D. Laing in Britain all offered versions of the same critique. Where the 19th- and early-20th-century bedlams were synonymous with neglect, physical restraint and cruelty, 'bins' for the unmanageable maniac, the modern mental hospitals were now seen as places of drug-induced zombification and conformity, psychological warfare, destruction of identity and, if necessary, psychiatrist gods implementing experimental or punitive treatments. As Laing wrote, 'In the best places, where straitjackets are abolished, doors unlocked, leucotomies largely forgone, these can be replaced by more subtle lobotomies and tranquillizers that place the bars of Bedlam *inside* the patient.' Arguments about the cultural construction of mental illness resonated, not least because amongst those who were admitted, certified and seen as in need of the radical psychiatric treatments of the era were gay people, victims of domestic abuse and women who had children outside marriage. The latter had their own specific clinical category of 'moral insanity'.

Laing and Basaglia were not just radical thinkers; they

were also committed to overturning psychiatric orthodoxy in practice. When Basaglia arrived as director of the obscure provincial asylum in Gorizia, near the Italian border with Yugoslavia, in 1961, he was appalled. The deprivation and ill-treatment were extreme. The 600-patient 'manicomio' smelt of 'death, of shit'. Patients were force-fed, sedated and restrained. The most difficult were kept in cages or strapped to beds with holes in them through which they relieved themselves. All the wards were locked, most patients were there involuntarily and treatment was mainly in the form of ECT and insulin shock therapy. Basaglia, who had been imprisoned for anti-fascist activism during the war, was reminded of Nazi concentration camps. In Italy, this comparison had a particular resonance. Mussolini had used the asylums to detain political opponents and suppress dissent. Patients, usually Jews, had been deported to the death camps.

Basaglia quickly became convinced that the system needed to be abolished entirely. Influenced by Laing's experiments at Kingsley Hall in east London and Maxwell Jones's at Dingleton Hospital in Melrose, Scotland, he began to remodel Gorizia as a therapeutic community. Power over the organisation of the asylum was devolved to the patients and decisions over its governance made at large open meetings. Patients could refuse treatment and venture outside the asylum walls, with some free to leave entirely. *L'istituzione negata* or *The Negated Institution*, published in 1968, which described the transformation at Gorizia, became a bestseller and brought fame to Basaglia and his project. Radicals saw in Gorizia a model for the reformation of society as a whole, one in which repressive structures and authorities – of the state, of institutions, of education, of the family, of religion and culture, of capitalism itself – would be torn down and replaced by a new liberatory order. Basaglia's ideas and those of the Psichiatria Democratica movement that formed around him gained mainstream traction, and in 1978 the Italian parliament passed Law 180 – better known as the Basaglia Law – which mandated the closure of all psychiatric hospitals, to be replaced with treatment and rehabilitation outside the hospital system.

But Basaglia is perhaps best remembered for a more symbolic act. In early 1973, when he was director of the San Giovanni Hospital in Trieste, he gave a group of artists and performers, including his cousin Vittorio and experimental theatre practitioner Giuliano Scabia, free run of the place. They established a 'laboratory' in one of the old wards, where patients, doctors, nurses and students were all encouraged to contribute creative ideas. One patient told the story of Marco Cavallo, the horse employed to pull the hospital laundry cart. When Marco grew too old to work the patients had successfully petitioned city authorities to save him from the slaughterhouse and allow dignified retirement to a farm. Over the following weeks a new Marco took shape in the laboratory, a four-metre-high, papier mâché sculpture of a horse painted bright blue and mounted on a trolley. Patients placed messages describing their hopes and dreams in the horse's belly. On 25 March he was ready. 'This is an important moment,' said Scabia. 'Marco Cavallo is about to leave. And the whole madhouse will leave with him.'

In the popular but disputed version of the story Marco Cavallo was too large to get through the door of the ward and so the wall was torn down to allow him to leave the hospital. Four hundred patients accompanied him through the asylum gates, down the hill and through the streets of Trieste. Basaglia saw the moment as explicitly symbolic: 'It is necessary at this stage that the external world recognises the psychiatric hospital as its own, and that a connection is made between an institution which is helping to rehabilitate people and a society which desires rehabilitation.' In another telling of the story, Marco Cavallo was a Trojan horse in reverse, 'wheeled from inside a walled compound to the outside, not to invade and capture a city but to free captives'.

A grainy, colour-saturated, Super 8 film of the event produced by Psichiatria Democratica shows patients emerging tentatively onto the front steps of the asylum and out into the light. Some grip the handrail, others are helped down the steps, someone carries a patient in a wheelchair. As Marco Cavallo is pulled along on ropes, people gather in procession around him or stand on the platform between his legs. Others play marching drums, or wave giant puppets and flags, as passers-by turn to look. Marco himself is bright blue, lean and angular, almost cubist. His left leg is planted forward, his neck extended and his head slightly upturned towards the sky. His mouth is open in a way that suggests a cry of pain or perhaps of defiance. Whatever the immediate symbolic or therapeutic impact of Marco Cavallo's procession through Trieste, the event quickly passed into myth. A bronze statue of Marco stands in the grounds of what was the San Giovanni asylum and his image became the symbol of mental health services in the city. Another replica, in the original blue, still tours the world, appearing at events as a symbol of liberation from oppression.

A more mainstream manifestation of the anti-psychiatric mood came in 1975 with the film of Ken Kesey's novel *One Flew Over the Cuckoo's Nest*, in which sadistic Nurse Ratched goes to war with the charismatic rebel McMurphy, played by Jack Nicholson. McMurphy is not ill – just a brawler and non-conformist who has feigned madness so that he could be transferred from a prison farm, where he had been sent after being convicted of rape – and neither, it turns out, are most of the other patients, or at least not really. In one of the key moments McMurphy discovers to his disgust that most of them are in hospital voluntarily and could leave at any time. They are not confined by law but because the system has so robbed them of autonomy and self-belief, or, as Kesey puts it explicitly in the novel, emasculated them. Asylums were not just asylums but metaphors for wider systems of control. It was not the people in them who were mad or bad but the places themselves, and by extension society itself. The film's director Miloš Forman identified with *One Flew Over the Cuckoo's Nest* when he read the script because he said it reminded him of Czechoslovakia under communism. Others, like Kesey, claimed it was a metaphor for the madness of capitalism, although the rampant misogyny of the novel suggests he saw another problem – the hero is a rapist, after all. The film climaxes with McMurphy finally subdued, destroyed by a lobotomy, the quintessentially modern form of medicine as torture, of state violence towards the individual. It did not matter that by the time of the film's release, its vision of psychiatric care was well out of date. There was certainly abuse and neglect but many of the radical treatments of the post-war period, including lobotomy, had been phased out.

Russell Barton, the new physician superintendent at Severalls, differed from many of the anti-psychiatry radicals in that he still believed in the potential of psychiatric hospitals to improve the health of patients, and what he proposed was a modern form of moral treatment. In his first year at Severalls he unlocked wards, removed the iron railings around the airing courts, brought in unrestricted visiting, built an industrial unit where patients could work, found employment for twenty-five more outside the hospital and decertified 800 of them altogether. Barton's aims were humane: 'to improve patients' contact with the outside world; the provision of useful occupation to every patient; the adoption of an attitude of encouragement and friendliness to each patient without foolish concessions; an emphasis on the quality of personal life of patients; a reduction of drugs'.

Barton also brought in art and music therapy. Patients were provided with Orff instruments, where the so-called devil's interval had been removed, the F and the B, allowing them to improvise together and never be out of tune. In 1967 he created a mother and baby unit so that newborns would not be separated from their sick mothers. Barton was also evangelical about the therapeutic benefits of physical exercise. In *Institutional Neurosis* he had written, in particular, about hula-hooping and this was put into practice at Severalls: 'We had hula-hoop groups for the very chronic... first of all the nurse would do it on her wrist, then she would hold the patient's hand and they would do it together, and then... the patient would do it on her own. Then the nurse would do it round her middle and then the patients would try it – it took them a long time to do it. Eventually there were whole wards of people hula-hooping. It was crazy.'

I do not remember when I found out that my father had been an inpatient at Severalls but it had never seemed like a secret. He talked freely and unprompted about it, and with an air of wonder, as if he couldn't quite believe it had happened. He meant to write it all down, I had heard him say several times over the years, but never had. He was happy, perhaps gratified, when I said I wanted to write about it myself.

He told these stories with relish and humour but – I can see this clearly now – it cannot have seemed very funny at the time. He was still young. The upward, aspirational trajectory of his life – grammar school, Oxford, academia – had been abruptly, perhaps catastrophically, stalled and the future must now have appeared utterly uncertain. What must he have thought, lying in his ward with Joe and Cliff and Bryan, waiting for my mother to visit or for the doctors to tell him what was going to happen to him, or, in the mornings, pumped full of insulin and waiting to see if he would have a seizure; how deeply strange and distressing life had suddenly become. In *Institutional Neurosis*, Russell Barton wrote: 'It is not easy to achieve one's identity and role in this life – where a role is defined as learned behaviour in relation to other people. This role, as a husband, wife, father, mother, neighbour, employee, member of different groups and so forth, disappears on admission to hospital.' My father had crossed a line, gone over into a world where few expect to go – a place still stigmatised enough that although his father visited him there, his mother would not. Would he lose his job or be unable to work altogether? In addition, my mother had discovered she was pregnant. 'Everyone thought we were crazy,' she says, to have a child when my father was so unwell.

One of Barton's enthusiasms was for group therapy. Every afternoon, following the insulin injections in the morning, my father sat in a large circle with many of his fellow patients, 'most of them drug addicts', he says. Asked to describe it, my father refers to the therapy scenes in *One Flew Over the Cuckoo's Nest*, which he had watched a few years after his own hospital stay with a sense of gleeful recognition. In one of them Nurse Ratched asks the rest of the group to comment on another patient's inability to sexually satisfy his wife. The other patients goad him until the session descends into chaos, to Nurse Ratched's apparent satisfaction. In another scene she asks Billy Bibbit to explain why he never told his mother he had asked a girl to marry him. 'Billy,' she says, pressing him to confess in front of the group, 'wasn't that the first time you tried to commit suicide?' In reality, my father said, the tea lady on his ward was a more effective confidante to many of the patients than any of the professionals. My father told her about my mother's pregnancy. 'So you've still got some strength left in you,' she said, cheerfully.

On another day, my father remembers, Lord Snowdon, Princess Margaret's husband at that time, arrived on the ward to take photos for a feature in *The Sunday Times Magazine*. Cliff, who had been self-harming, objected to having his picture taken. 'Well,' said Barton, 'you can't complain. You did it to yourself.' To the patients this celebrity visit must have seemed like just the latest surreal twist in their hospital experience, enough to convince them of their unsteady grip on reality, perhaps. In fact, I have not been able to find any official record of the visit or the pictures that resulted. My mother thought she had kept the article but couldn't find it. Snowdon himself offers some corroboration. In an interview thirty years later he described how *The Sunday Times* sent him and the journalist Marjorie Wallace – later the founder of the mental health charity SANE – to look at the conditions in psychiatric hospitals. 'We used to go into mental institutions at five or six in the morning when you just had the night staff and you were more likely to get in.' Once in, Wallace would distract the staff whilst Snowdon darted into the wards with his Leica. At Severalls, it seems highly plausible that Barton would have welcomed them and shown them around himself.

The world outside was in its own kind of fever and at times news penetrated the hospital. One morning near the beginning of my father's stay, as he and others lay in bed waiting for an insulin seizure, a nurse rushed in. 'Bobby Kennedy's been shot!' he announced. Nurse Beaney was taking everyone's blood pressure and the results were all off the scale. Weeks later – by which time my father was a day patient – the same nurse appeared again. 'The Russians have invaded Czechoslovakia!' he shouted.

Beneath the comedy of his stories, however, what my father really felt was contempt. Contempt for the psychiatrists, these high-minded reformers, their hubris and arrogance. Contempt for their continued belief in quack cures. Contempt, in particular, for Dr Fox – 'a chief in his little fiefdom', my father said. Prior to his admission to Severalls my father had been put on Valium for his nerves. Dr Fox thought it would be a good idea to get him off it. 'We could go cold turkey but I wouldn't like to be there to see it,' Fox said. Nevertheless, one day my father noticed that his pills had changed colour. When he queried it, he was told that they had switched his Valium with vitamin C without telling him.

My father never had a 'reaction' to the treatment, although he saw patients in the beds around him have seizures. After five weeks of injections there was another consultation with Dr Fox and a number of the other staff. The ward nurse told Fox what dose of insulin my father was on. As my father recalls it, Fox went pale. 'I think we'd better pull it back a bit,' he said. The treatment went on for a few more days and then ended. A few days after that my father was discharged and became a day patient on the basis that his condition had improved. He did feel a little better, he says, but does not attribute this to the treatment he received. The only obvious legacy of the modified insulin therapy was that, as a result of his supercharged appetite, he – always a thin man – was now fat. Soon afterwards, new research concluded that the treatment was dangerous and ineffective, and it was discontinued.

In the autumn my father went back to work and although still unwell he was able to carry on, using the camp bed in his office as before, and never missed a lecture or a tutorial. The unrest at the university had died down but its reputation for radicalism persisted and by some accounts did long-term damage to its prospects. My father continued to have psychotherapy, but didn't find it much help. A young doctor in the village told him, 'Well, of course there is always one way out,' which my father took to mean suicide. My brother was born in the spring of 1969 and I came five years later. Our early childhood in the village was happy, idyllic even. If my father's illness cast any shadows, my brother and I were not aware of them. My parents had many friends and my mother supported my father when he needed it, as he would support her later. Neither of them expected to see Severalls again.

PART THREE

If I stay here, I shall lose my mind

I

BEVERLEY, MY CONTACT IN THE DEVELOPER'S SALES office at Kingswood Heath, explained on the phone that at this stage it would only be possible to see the show homes on the development, not one of the houses that was actually available to buy. That would require evidence of being in a 'proceedable position', such as very close to selling my current house or with a mortgage deal approved. I assumed this was to discourage time-wasters and voyeurs, and this did not seem unreasonable given my own motivations.

Severalls was being erased, disappearing in front of my eyes as I had walked around the site, connections to the past it embodied being severed. I had not managed to enter the site as a curious visitor, or as a trespasser, my brief encounter with the workman aside, and in this sense the place seemed as enclosed and impenetrable as it had ever been. But this was another way in, to style myself as a house buyer, someone invested in the future of the place rather than the past. I toyed, briefly, with the idea of enlisting Ellie to come with me, to double down on the fiction of a family looking to buy a new home, but this would mean telling her what I had in mind. I still had not mentioned these trips to her, let alone to my parents. The whole enterprise – whatever it was – remained covert, slightly shameful, ridiculous even.

I dressed to make myself seem credible, as I imagined someone would if they really were interested in buying a house – my smartest shoes, no jeans, a shirt and a jacket. I had bought a house myself, of course, several years before and doubted whether I had got dressed up for the experience. This made me wonder, as I sat on the train to Colchester, if, in fact, it might have the opposite effect, whether my outfit radiated insincerity, advertised me as someone who had no real intention of buying a house. I made notes for what seemed a plausible backstory, a slight counterfactual that was close enough to the truth that it would not be such a stretch for me to inhabit. I had grown up near Colchester and had just got a job at the university. I was married with two children, a girl and a boy, and although I would be commuting from London at first, the long-term plan was for the whole family to relocate. We wanted four bedrooms, a generous garden. The development appealed because of its location, its proximity to the A12, and because I knew and liked the area from when I was at school. I made a list of questions, the sort it seemed like a genuine buyer might ask, which I had once asked myself: about schools and shops and council tax and when the houses would be available to move into.

My anxieties were unnecessary, I knew. There was no way of proving that I did not want to buy a house on Kingswood

Heath and, even if there were, no crime was being committed. It was all harmless and victimless, except for a small amount of Beverley's time. Nevertheless, although I had earlier dismissed the idea of a criminal entry into the site, as the train pulled in at Colchester, this alternative plan felt barely less unnerving.

This time I took the bus from the station and got off on Via Urbis Romanae, directly outside the sales office. Next to it hung the banner of the family holding hands, walking down the country lane. Along the verge the daffodils that that were blooming on my last visit had gone but the elm saplings had grown taller. As it turned out, Beverley was not available. When I gave my name, she looked up from the other side of the office and waved. She was sitting with a group of people, three generations of the same family it seemed, going through some paperwork, and the mood of excitement, even giddiness, suggested they had just made a big decision. Instead, I was escorted out by Alice, a younger saleswoman – more junior, it seemed to me – and this was vaguely disappointing.

There were a range of properties available on the development and an example of each stood in a short strip just beyond the office. On the phone to Beverley I had expressed interest in 'The Orford', a £460,000 four-bedroom house described in the brochure as 'offering contemporary living over three floors, stylish sanitary-ware, contemporary style Symphony fitted kitchens with soft close doors and drawers', and this was where we started. Alice and I took our shoes off at the door and put on white cotton slippers of the kind sometimes provided along with a towelling bathrobe in hotels. She asked me if I had ever been to one of their homes before and explained that they were higher-spec and more spacious than those of their competitors, certainly on this development. 'It's a family-run company,' she said.

Alice led the way. She was friendly enough but I felt immediately that selling houses was not her passion. As we padded from room to room I paused for what seemed like a reasonable amount of time in each. I commented on the good size of the rooms, although they were in fact very modest, and the practicality of the layout. I tried the taps, flexed the door handles and the toilet flushes. I ran my finger along the grain of the windowsill and inspected the windows themselves. Alice emphasised the advantages of buying a new build – everything works, highly energy efficient, a two-year guarantee if there are any problems. If I were to buy one still in the early stages of construction I would be able to use the 'Your Choice' personalisation guide to select from a range of finishes for the kitchen, bathroom and en suite.

Her delivery was functional, automatic, as if she was thinking about something else. She asked me no questions about myself or my situation, even though I did my best to invite them, and all this – like Beverley's unavailability – was obscurely disappointing. As I continued to comment on and praise the house I had the sense of my own behaviour as not only repetitive, my checking of the taps and turning of door handles, but increasingly insincere and theatrical. A more engaged salesperson, I felt, might have noticed this performance and been curious, even suspicious, but Alice seemed unaware, and this had the effect of making me try to prove myself even more – lingering for longer in each room, asking more and more questions. Once we got to the kitchen, and I had admired the soft-closing action of the cupboards and drawers, I asked if there had been a lot of interest in the houses, and at this she brightened up.

'Oh yes,' she said, 'we've been run off our feet. Since Chelmsford got city status people have been priced out of there. And Colchester is much more desirable than Ipswich, although it's only twenty minutes away. I don't really under-stand that.' She paused. 'I live in Ipswich.'

Colchester would not be a bad place to move to, to live. As Alice had suggested, plenty of people seemed to feel that way. The town is booming. By some estimates – cer-tainly its own – it is the fastest growing town in the country, the population rising from 155,000 to 190,000 in the last twenty years. The appeal was fairly obvious. Less hectic than London but only an hour away on the train, not too big but not too small, some good schools, cheaper than else-where. It had its aesthetic, cultural and lifestyle advantages, too. The developer's brochure made much of the town's long history, its status as Britain's oldest recorded town and Roman capital, the well-preserved Norman castle, as well as proximity to the Essex coast and 'the stunning Dedham Vale Area of Outstanding Natural Beauty, celebrated in the paintings of John Constable'.

The borough council has been a fervent evangelist for this boom, trumpeting the area as a 'three billion pound investment hotspot'. On one of its promotional websites, under the slogan 'Colchester – Ultra Ready for Business', counters keep a live tally of the numbers of homes built, jobs created, millions invested. In 2011 the £28 million art gallery Firstsite opened on the site of the old bus station in the newly christened 'Creative Quarter'. A piece of metallic, angular modernism designed by celebrity Uruguayan architect Rafael Viñoly, it was another statement of civic intent. In the summer of 2018, as part of its effort to promote tourism to the town, the council paid £40,000 for a thirty-second advert on Sky TV.

The boom in Colchester is not popular with everyone and many of the developments have proved controversial. People argue that much of the new housing is ugly and poor quality, that the town's infrastructure cannot handle it, that the council is in thrall to the developers or profiteering for short-term gain. The money is certainly flowing but there is the sense of a place trying too hard. The town, or at least its boosters, seem to have a chip on their shoulder about not being something more, an inferiority complex about Chelmsford. Firstsite is often cited as evidence of this. Criticised from the beginning for its cost and design, and the fact that it had no permanent collection, the curves and slopes of the building make it uniquely difficult to stage exhibitions or hang things from the walls. It achieved national notoriety when a report by local activists claimed that the majority of its visitors were only entering the building to use the toilets. In response, the gallery's director argued that it was 'not possible to say any visit is definitively non-cultural'.

I looked out into the back garden of The Orford – a meagre, fenced-in space, newly turfed. I tried to imagine the asylum, as it had once been, the large-windowed, high-ceilinged Edwardian hospital building and villas, the sports fields, the generous and beautifully kept grounds, the farm, the bakehouse, the laundry, the social club and the dance hall.

'It might be perfect for us,' I said, 'with the kids.'

Alice did not react to this but went back into the hall and knelt down to take her slippers off, and I followed her.

'I grew up near here,' I said, 'in Wivenhoe.'

'I've heard of it,' she said. 'Shall we move on?'

Next door was 'The Bredon', detached with four bedrooms but only single fronted, for £360,000. We took our shoes off at the door and put on new slippers. We went round more quickly this time, more or less in silence. In the living room two framed prints were hung on a greeny-blue-painted wall, above a beige sofa. One read, in large italics, 'It's Good to Be Home,' and on the other was a cross section of half a lime and, in the same font, 'Let the Evening Begin.'

'This used to be the Severalls Hospital site, didn't it?' I said.

I'd been saving this up and had some idea she would deny this or plead ignorance, but she didn't.

'Yes,' Alice said, and again her interest seemed to flicker a little, 'and the grounds are lovely. We've retained a lot of trees.'

I nodded but now that the question had been answered so straightforwardly, I couldn't think how to follow it up.

'Do you want to see any others?' Alice said, the enthusiasm gone again.

I told her it was fine. I thanked her and we shook hands on the doorstep of The Bredon. The viewings had lasted no more than twenty minutes, although it had felt like longer. It all seemed to have fizzled out, weighed down by the lack of conviction on both sides. As she turned away, I said, 'What would be the next stage, if I were to...'

'Oh yes,' said Alice, 'I should have said. If you want to formally express an interest we need to see evidence of an approved mortgage deal.' She gave me her card and smiled brightly, happy to be concluding things. 'Contact the office at any time.'

Beyond the show homes were four short streets of the finished houses, a combination of Orfords, Bredons and others I did not know the names of. They were all variations on a theme, some with three bedrooms, some with four, some single fronted, some double fronted, some two storeys, one of them three storeys, some in red brick, others finished with a speckled off-white plaster facade – but somehow this only emphasised the sense of maximum, off-the-peg architectural blandness. I saw no people. The signs of occupation were there – a car in the driveway, a child's tricycle by the front door – but even these seemed like props, part of some orchestrated scene rather than anything natural or authentic. As I walked, I felt a dense air of unreality, as if I were in a virtual re-creation of the place rather than the real thing, a mirage or projection that might suddenly, without warning, flicker out. Perhaps all new developments carry this sense of eeriness, this provisionality. The streets and streets of Victorian terraces that seem so elemental to London had once been building sites, improbable and awkward additions to the landscape. Severalls, too, when it was being built, when its endless corridors, offices and wards, the main hall, the villas and the water tower were being grafted onto the woods and fields, when thousands of visitors streamed around it in May 1913, would have seemed bright and new but somehow hard to believe in. It, too, would have taken time to acquire depth and weight, beyond the evangelism and boosterism of the Lunacy Commission, the Board of Control and the county council.

I walked up and down the four streets. I looked again at the houses and tried to imagine myself wanting to live there. I thought of the family I had seen in the office, in the process of buying one of these houses, or one identical to them. Their excitement had been clear, and this newness, this blank slate, this depthlessness, presumably spoke differently to them. They were engaged together in this collective enterprise – grandparents helping out with the deposit, young parents getting their name on the mortgage, children excited for a new home, more space, perhaps the garden they hadn't had – driving the family forward into the future.

I thought of the oddness of my being here, the inexplicability, really. I thought, again, of the former patients who, long after the closure of the hospital, still sometimes turned up, bewildered by the changes. I pictured them walking down these new streets looking for signs of the place they had known, and wondered what they would make of them. And then I had another odd idea, a brief sensation really, quickly dismissed: that I had come because, in fact, I did want to buy one of these houses, that at some impossible-to-fathom level I did want to live here; that instead of tricking Beverley and Alice by making this journey, I had tricked myself.

I was surprised, over the next couple of weeks, to receive several voicemails from Alice asking me if I was still interested in the properties. I didn't return her calls.

2

WHEN I WAS YOUNGER, MY FATHER'S TIME IN
hospital had always seemed to me to be a discrete and distant moment in time, a bizarre interlude in life – life before
I was born – that had no wider legacy or relevance. As a
child, I had always been aware of the bottle of pills that rattled against the keys in his pocket, brown tinted glass with
a white cap, but it never occurred to me to ask about it.
Even if I had, the answer – it contained Valium – would not
have meant anything to me; perhaps all fathers had them.
However, my mother's admission to Severalls, sixteen years
later, was something altogether different.

I only went there once when my mother was an inpatient
– or only once that I remember. The details are sketchy, possibly unreliable, but I know that the visit was not a success.
It was the summer of 1984, when I was nine, about to be
ten, and the plan was to take my mother out for the day, or
at least for a few hours. I did not go into the hospital building but waited in the car whilst my father went to collect her.
My image of the place is disappointingly thin – a car park, a

large building, a sunny day. I do not remember my brother being there, although it seems odd that he would not have been. He remembers visiting but does not remember me being there either. Perhaps my father had decided it was better – for us? For my mother? – if we only visited her one at a time.

My father brought my mother out to the car and we drove out of the hospital, away from Colchester and the village where we now lived, towards Dedham, where my parents had lived when they were first married and when my father was admitted to hospital. Almost immediately, my mother became paranoid and insisted that her doctors were following us in a white car behind. I remember turning around in the back seat, the curving, leafy country roads, a bridge over a river, willows on the banks, to see if what she was saying was true. My father tried to reassure her but she would not be calmed down. Eventually he lost his temper, as he only rarely did, stopped the car and turned around. We drove her back and the visit was abandoned.

When I was unwell myself, around twenty-five years later, on one of the days that my mother came to London to look after me, she brought up her own illness. 'We've never talked much about it, have we?' she said. I forget what, if anything, had prompted her to say this, but my own crisis had taken some layers off everyone and enforced a new intimacy between us. It was true we hadn't really talked about her illness. But it was difficult, painful, a long time ago. Why would we? I started to cry. 'It's OK,' I said to her, 'everything makes me cry at the moment,' and this was true, too.

Much later, sometime after our visit to the old Severalls site, my mother gave me a folder labelled, in her own hand-writing, 'Confidential MOOD DISORDER RESEARCH'. She told me then that in 2010 she had agreed to take part in a research project by the University of Birmingham and the University of Cardiff. A researcher came to interview her at home and at their request she also wrote a three-page 'Summary of Mental Health', a condensed history of her life – or at least that aspect of it – from 1961 onwards. The docu-ment was divided into sections titled, 'First Depression', 'Second Depression', 'First Manic Episode', 'Second Manic Episode', and so on. It was signed and dated, giving it the formal feel of a witness statement or a confession, which in a way I suppose it was.

There was no obvious trigger or trauma at the root of my mother's illness. She was the oldest of three siblings from a loving, stable home in south-east London. During her teens and twenties, my mother wrote, she had little self-confidence but this was covered up by an ability to get on with people and make friends easily. She was bright and academically minded, winning a scholarship to the local high school before going on to study botany, geology and zoology at Reading University. Just prior to her final exams there in 1961, she had her first depressive episode following a break-up with a boyfriend. She was supported by friends and didn't go to the doctor. From Reading she went to work as a research assistant at Leicester University, where she met my father, who was doing a PhD. On field trips to the Lake District she gathered samples, which she boiled up in the lab to identify pollen grains, an early form of what would become climate science. She was alone in the lab and found the work boring and isolating, and following a break-up with my father, she had another depressive episode. When she wasn't in the lab she was in bed. In particular, she remembers lying there for hours in January 1965 listening to Winston Churchill's funeral on the radio.

In the spring of that year she had her first manic episode. It was like a switch being turned on, she wrote. One Saturday morning she got up early and cleaned her car before breakfast. She started spending money. My parents were back together by this point and my father remembers her emerging from the university bookshop weighed down with an enormous pile of books. She annoyed her supervisor by singing whilst she worked in the lab, and on trips to the Lake District she bought endless things from the gift shops. In the summer she organised a large party to which she invited all the students and academics she knew, something she would never previously have been bold enough to do.

My mother gradually came down from this high and there followed a period of calm, at least in terms of her own health. My parents got married, moved to Essex and started work at the university. When my father became unwell, the fear that he might one day have to give up work weighed on her, but my mother coped and my brother and I were born. In 1981 she got what seemed like her dream job, working in the offices of a celebrated garden designer, but within two years it had gone sour. Her boss, the gardener, was a tyrant and a bully, and following an argument my mother resigned. 'I felt that my world had fallen apart,' she wrote in her summary, 'as though the cork had come out of a lemonade bottle'. This marked the beginning of her 'Third Depression', the first since my brother and I had been born, and the most severe.

3

IF THE HEYDAY OF SEVERALLS AND THE ASYLUM system had already passed when my father was an inpatient, by 1984, when my mother was admitted, it was a relic, well into its long decline. The reforms of Russell Barton and others like him around the country in the 1960s and 1970s were a last gasp of these institutions as well as a herald of the new drive towards de-institutionalisation. The political will to support the old system had gone, replaced by the rhetoric – if not the reality – of 'community care' and the imperative of cost-cutting. The Victorian and Edwardian estates were vast, crumbling, expensive to maintain and unsuitable for modern methods of treatment. The public exposures of cruelty and neglect kept coming and the new generation of drugs appeared to further undermine the case for accommodating mentally ill people in the same way.

At Severalls, Russell Barton's knack for attracting controversy had increasingly put him at odds with his employers. In 1967 Barbara Robb had published *Sans Everything*, a scathing report on the treatment of elderly people in hospitals.

Barton wrote the foreword to the book, in which he reiterated some of the arguments of *Institutional Neurosis*, arguing that institutions 'develop powerful instruments of defence for their protection and perpetuation' and that the care of patients often became subordinate to that. His superiors in the regional health board and in government were unimpressed.

The following year, the summer that my father was in Severalls, Barton allowed the journalist Irma Kurtz, posing as a patient, to enter the hospital admissions ward in order to gather material for an article published later in the year in *Nova* magazine. This looked like a perverse attempt to stitch up his own institution but in fact the article is, at least at a distance of fifty years, remarkably measured, humane, disappointingly free of sensational detail. Kurtz described an environment where the greatest threat was not abuse or neglect – the nurses she met were uniformly kind and cheerful – nor maniac patients, but sheer institutionally sanctioned boredom: 'The big clock on the wall lingered over every third minute just as my school clock used to; someone coughed, lit a cigarette, sighed; in the distance somewhere I heard sound of activity but already I had been lulled by inertia and I felt a great reluctance to lift myself from the chair. "If I stay here," Mrs O whispered to me, "I shall lose my mind."'

Myland Court, one of the villas set away from the main building amongst the gardens, where Kurtz was resident for three days, was home to the most mildly afflicted of the patients and known to the rest of the hospital as 'The

Holiday Camp'. According to Kurtz, patients discussed the suicide attempts that had got them admitted and some were carted off periodically for ECT, but displays of florid madness were absent. Elsewhere, on a visit to the main canteen, where patients from different wards mixed freely, and to a locked ward, Kurtz saw the more acute cases, but the regime itself still appeared benign, or at least as benign as it could be. Overall, though, Kurtz's abiding impression was not of otherness but of the flimsily constructed division between those inside the hospital and those out, the mad and the not mad: 'I pictured everyone I knew or knew about... and there was not one, not a single one, who couldn't have slipped down the long corridors of Severalls as easily as I myself was doing. From the serenity of Myland Court, it looked a knife-edge we walk outside with our sleeping tablets, heavy drinking, guilt, aspirins, debt, chocolate, and our secret tears.' The thinking here feels very much in sync with the times, even if the idiosyncrasy of the list – chocolate! aspirins! – makes it feel like an itemisation of her own vices.

Nevertheless, the regional hospital board saw Barton's unilateral decision to let Kurtz in and risk exposing the hospital to media attack as a further example of his arrogance and irresponsibility, and an inquiry concluded that he had shown bad judgement. At the time of Barton's appointment as the physician superintendent, the power invested in that role was still more or less absolute. It was possible for a visionary to impose his vision, but in the process Barton had made many enemies. A merger with general hospital services in the area started to erode his power and he was in constant conflict with central government, the group committee and other members of staff. The relationship between Barton and Dr Fox, whom Barton had appointed as a consultant five years earlier, had also become poisonous, a 'clash of two monumental egos' observed another member of staff. In 1969 Fox told the regional hospital board that he suspected Barton of wanting to murder him. Barton later sued Fox for libel and won, but by then the board had already abolished the role of physician superintendent and he had been forced out of Severalls.

By 1985, in England and Wales the average number of occupied beds in psychiatric hospitals had declined steeply to 64,800 from a high of 148,100 in 1954. Huge numbers of so-called long-stay patients had been moved 'into the community' – a euphemism which covered everything from a mishmash of vastly inadequate services to being returned to family or being made homeless. With a few exceptions, the fate of these formerly chronic patients was not tracked or recorded. And yet despite this, and despite the 1962 Hospital Plan, which explicitly mandated the closure of the UK's psychiatric hospitals, by the mid-1980s all of the major hospitals were still open. In fact, the number of admissions to psychiatric hospitals had gone up but with patients staying for much shorter periods, many of them on a repeated basis. Overall, the picture was confusing, the long-term fate of individual institutions unclear.

In *The Last Asylum*, Barbara Taylor describes the experience of being an inpatient at Friern Hospital, the old Colney

Hatch asylum, in this limbo period. She was admitted in 1989 and though Friern didn't close for another half decade, the place already seemed to her like 'a bloody museum': 'I look around at the peeling paint, the dirty windows, the ancient, scabby brick. The reception desk is a mahogany cubbyhole with a broken ivory bell... What a hellhole.' The hospital was more than half empty, the number of patients down from 3,000 in the 1950s to 800. Taylor's ward, designed for more than fifty, now had twenty-seven: 'Patients and staff rattled around like pebbles in a vacuum flask.'

All over the country the picture was similar – these once monumental institutions denuded of services and staff with wards closed and patient numbers shrunk, politically and publicly unloved, apparently doomed. Nevertheless, they persisted, the result of bureaucratic inertia and the lack of anything substantial to put in their place, a zombie system that would not quite die. It was often only in the individual hospitals themselves and their immediate communities that there was regret for this state of affairs. In July 1983 staff at Friern learned from a television news announcement that the hospital was to be closed. They began a vigorous campaign to keep it open and enlisted patients, former patients, a local MP and the vicar for the area, amongst others, to the cause.

Severalls' history over this period mirrored the experience at Friern – declining patient numbers, an uncertain future, the shift towards managerialism. It was absorbed into the area health authority system and the hospital management committees were abolished. At the same time new community care facilities were set up, with voluntary organisations providing shared housing for some former long-stay patients. In the 1980s cuts and changes to mental health policy accelerated the hospital's decline, although, like Friern, it was still more than a decade before it would finally close its doors.

Occasionally Severalls appeared in the news, usually for sensational reasons that often involved Dr Fox. The hospital had long operated a policy of taking a small number of patients from Broadmoor and Rampton high-security psychiatric hospitals before releasing them back into the community. In 1977 Alan Roy Murphy, who had been transferred from Rampton, was convicted of killing Estelle Noble, a fellow patient at Severalls. The policy was suspended, to the regret of Fox, who was quoted in the local paper: 'It's a setback but it should not mean the end of the scheme.' Also in 1977 Hupadoo Vencatasamy, a nurse, was detained at Severalls following the fatal poisoning of one of his daughters. In 1979, on Fox's recommendation, he was released and given a job at the Turner Village Hospital for the mentally handicapped in Colchester as part of his rehabilitation. When his background was revealed after only a few days and he was sacked, he killed himself and another of his daughters with carbon monoxide piped from the exhaust of his car. Fox described the inquest that followed as 'half-baked' but resigned anyway, citing general frustration with the NHS. 'The scope for medical innovation and control has passed,' he said, 'and I believe I can achieve more – before senility sets in – in a place where chief of service means precisely that.' He took a job in New York, insisting that he would not return to Colchester, although he did. In 2000 he was back in the local news, having provided a psychiatric report recommending that a man suffering from body dysmorphia be granted his wish to have his left leg amputated.

Russell Barton's own post-Severalls trajectory reads as something of a cautionary tale. His bridges burnt in the UK, Barton also went to the US, to become superintendent of a state-run psychiatric hospital in Rochester, Upstate New York, where he died in 2002, aged seventy-eight. In a curious twist, in as much as his legacy endures, at least online, it is as a co-opted propagandist for Holocaust denial. In 1945 Barton had been one of a group of medical student volunteers who had entered Belsen concentration camp two weeks after its liberation to help survivors, an experience which informed his decision to become a psychiatrist and the particular shape of his professional interests. In 1968, whilst still at Severalls, he published an article in Purnell's *History of the Second World War* in which he compared the practices in Belsen to NHS psychiatric services. Barton asserted, based on his eyewitness experience but not on further research or corroboration, that the thousands of deaths at Belsen were the result not of a deliberate Nazi policy of starvation, but of acute overcrowding in the final year of the war. The article caused an immediate furore; *The Times* ran a scathing report under the headline 'Belsen "Not too bad"' and the row tainted Barton's reputation irreparably.

Much of the article was in fact a development of the ideas he had addressed in *Institutional Neurosis* and elsewhere – the erosion of identity and stigmatisation that takes place in an institutional setting; the way individual conscience was apt to be overruled by group loyalty to permit cruelty, ill-treatment, humiliation – at a time when the considerable abuses of the psychiatric system were still not officially recognised. Barton's later decisions, however, are harder to explain. The article was picked up by Holocaust deniers and cited as evidence that the official narrative of the death camps was a fabrication. Barton acted as witness for the defence in two prosecutions of Ernst Zündel, publisher of Richard Harwood's book *Did Six Million Really Die?*, in which he reiterated his opinion that there had been no deliberate policy of starvation at Belsen. In a video on YouTube – the only footage of Barton I have been able to find – under the title 'Holocaust Myth' you can see him interviewed by Zündel. Barton is white-haired, weary looking, uneasy, sitting cramped behind a small table against a cheap wooden partition, the whole scene bathed in a sickly yellow light.

4

DESPITE EVERYTHING I HAD READ ABOUT THE irreversible nature of chronic anxiety, for me things gradually got better. Being at work helped – the distraction, being busy, feeling that I was fulfilling my obligations and earning a living. The new house had begun to feel like home. I stopped spending so much time online. I took an Ativan when I needed one and the strips Chris sent through the post lasted longer. But two years later I broke down again. Following a week of intense headaches, sleeplessness and early waking, and the stiffness in my hands that had marked the beginning of the first episode, I began to unravel once more. I went back to the doctor, a different one now, and he switched me from citalopram to venlafaxine. Venlafaxine is a stronger antidepressant which works by a different mechanism and is used as a second-line treatment when SSRIs such as citalopram have not been effective. I paid for some counselling, better and more suited to me than that provided by the GP surgery, and this was helpful. I used Ativan liberally to keep me functioning and managed to keep working.

Overall, the crash was not quite so brutal and the recovery a little quicker. I stayed on the venlafaxine – which may or may not have been helping – but eased off the Ativan.

Around this time, on the train home after work, I ran into a friend I had not seen for more than ten years. Danny and I had known each other at university and started spending more time together after we had graduated and moved to London. I got him a job at the pub where I was working, a fun place where there were a lot of drugs and we gave free drinks to our friends. We played music together and had some big parties at the shared house I was living in. He was charismatic, a talented musician, full of energy and ideas, someone who drew people in. He was extreme, too – drinking heavily and then suddenly quitting to smoke huge amounts of weed instead. I'd heard some stories about him at university, that he had once locked himself in the toilet of his flat, refused to come out for a whole night, and written and drawn on the walls, but nothing that seemed to amount to very much. Then, one afternoon when I was at work he called the pub to ask if I could take his shift that evening. I couldn't and when he turned up a couple of hours later he seemed disorientated, following me around the bar whilst I served drinks. I still didn't think much of it, and when my shift finished I went home and only heard the rest later.

After I left, the pub started to get very busy, as it always did at that time, and Danny became too distressed to work. He stood at the end of the bar with his hands clenched together, paralysed as people clamoured for drinks. Someone took him into the garden, where he talked incoherently and wept. After a while he said he felt better and left on his bike, saying he was going home. He spent the next few hours cycling all over London, calling his family to say that he was being pursued. Eventually his sister met him at Waterloo and took him to hospital. A day or two later his parents arrived at his flat to pick up his things. I did not see him again until we bumped into each other on the train that day years later.

We were living nearby again, it turned out, now both in south London, and we arranged to go for a drink the following week. It was then that he filled in the gaps. For the first year, he told me, he did not come out of his room, refusing all visitors and phone calls. His mother took meals in to him and, every two weeks, a pack of Marlboro Lights. He would smoke one of these a day, stubbing it out after a few drags. He could not read the news or watch TV, believing that everything was part of an elaborate conspiracy to cause him harm. He could read novels published before he was born, however, because, he reasoned, none of these could be directed at him, and so this is what he did – vast amounts of Dickens, Tolstoy, Zola and others, though now he could remember none of it. The rest of the time, he lay staring at the posters on the walls of his teenage bedroom.

After a year or so, the doctors found a drug combination that lifted him off the bottom and he began to resume something like normal life – starting to cook, play his cello and his bass, and help around the house. After five years at home he moved into his own flat and started working again, as a graphic designer, and making new friends. He played in bands and acted in some plays. Despite this, he knew he was fragile. Every so often, someone from his old life would try to make contact and he would feel the danger in it, that the associations it triggered might easily bring him down. Earlier that evening he had wondered, he told me as we sat in the pub, whether he would come and meet me after all.

I was one of the people who had tried to make contact with him during those years. At the beginning I had called a few times and spoken to his mother. Then, periodically, I had sent him postcards when I was away, to try to let him know he wasn't forgotten, although I doubt now that this was helpful to him. For the first few years, I often thought of him, especially when there was something big, when friends we had in common started to get married or have children. It seemed an extraordinary thing to have just vanished from your own life in this way, a very sad thing, and I would think about where he was and what he was doing. So much had happened in my own life – I had met Ellie, travelled, had different jobs, started to write, had a child, got married, published a book. But I'd had a breakdown, too, and it seemed strange – even fated – that I would run into him now, when I was trying to make sense of things myself.

It was good to see him. He was off his medication now and feeling well. He still had the old charisma and intensity, and I remembered clearly why we had been friends. Talking to him put my own crisis into perspective, his own had been so much worse – a full psychotic break, heavy-duty medication, periods of hospitalisation, returning to live with his parents and then rebuilding his life more or less from scratch. Still, I felt a kinship with him, that we had touched or shared some form of experience that others had not, and we went on seeing each other from time to time. Our lives were different these days and he still did not want to see our other mutual friends, but it felt good to maintain this contact. It seemed somehow redemptive to rekindle our friendship, a reminder that things are not always lost.

In 2010, around four years after he had become ill with chronic fatigue syndrome, my father staged his own, much more dramatic recovery. One of the features of his illness – perhaps any amorphous, difficult-to-treat illness – was that there was always someone who knew someone who had recovered from it and was evangelical about the treatment that had helped them. And so, on the recommendation of my cousin's husband's sister, who had been diagnosed with chronic fatigue syndrome but was now fully recovered and back at work, my father signed up for a three-day residential course in Dorset. The treatment was very controversial in chronic fatigue circles because its method, which used theories of neuro-linguistic programming to alter patterns of behaviour, seemed to imply that the illness was essentially psychological (along with chronic fatigue sufferers, it was principally aimed at people with depression) and because it promised such transformative results. Consequently, passionate advocates who claimed to have seen or experienced such results themselves were ranged against other sufferers and the medical establishment, who saw it as cynical quackery that gave false hope and was designed to relieve vulnerable people of substantial amounts of money.

Such a recovery certainly seemed implausible, too much to hope for, and we were all sceptical, not least my father, who had previous experience of quacks and charlatans. The information available in advance did not give much away or inspire confidence, a blend of cultish and corporate propaganda, the name of the treatment heavily trademarked and the exact details seemingly a commercial secret. But my father had tried the conventional, recommended treatments without making progress. He was desperate, and willing to suspend disbelief. Aside from the money, there seemed little to lose.

My brother drove my mother and father to Dorset and three days later I went back with him to pick them up. I forget why we both went – to share the driving, I suppose, or more likely for moral support. The change in my father was immediately apparent. It was a lovely day, warm and bright and cloudless, and when we pulled into the driveway of the farmhouse where they had been staying, my parents were sitting around a table in the garden with seven or eight others. My brother and I were brought tea and cake and introduced to the group, who were all talking and smiling and laughing as if they were old friends. As my parents said their farewells there were promises to write and email and meet up again soon. My father's wheelchair was already folded up and leaning against a wall and he insisted on helping my brother and me to pack it into the boot of the car.

As we drove, my parents sitting in the back and my brother and I in the front, my father talked rapidly and almost non-stop. It was a stream of free association, jumping from one subject to another, his thoughts apparently moving more quickly than he could articulate. He commented on everything he could see out of the window as we drove – a vintage car that was similar to one his brother had once owned, a pub that might have been nice for lunch if it hadn't been past lunchtime, the way the countryside reminded him of a holiday he and my mother had taken before my brother and I were born. At times he seemed exhausted by his own efforts. He would try to stop himself, closing his eyes and taking deep breaths, his right arm placed across his chest so that his hand lay over his heart, like someone swearing an oath. At another point he took a small card from his wallet and began to mouth whatever was written on it, some kind of mantra it seemed. Throughout, his foot drummed on the floor of the car.

My brother dropped me at Guildford station so that I could catch the train home, whilst he drove my parents the rest of the way back to Essex. I went to the station toilets to take an Ativan and I remember then standing on the platform on the phone to Ellie, baffled and amazed, trying to convey the bizarreness of it all, my sense of what was possible entirely upended. The change was extreme, even troubling, as if he had been given too much of the necessary medicine. It did not seem sustainable. But over the following days – as we gathered from talking to him and my mother – the mania passed but my father's renewed energy remained. He started sleeping back upstairs and eating meals with my mother in the dining room or in front of the TV. They went out to see friends and started making plans for trips and holidays. They gave the wheelchair to a friend who needed it. A few months later the stairlift that had ferried my father to the upstairs bathroom was dismantled and moved into the garage.

The feeling of having witnessed something close to a miracle was enhanced by the fact that my father remained enigmatic about the treatment itself – what was involved, how it was supposed to work and what this meant about his illness. At times he retreated to the bedroom where, we gathered, he enacted some ritual sequence of movements and mantras designed to re-establish or reinforce his well-being, but when we asked him directly he was vague or said that he would explain properly at some point in the future. It seemed that this was on the instruction of the therapist who ran the course – 'a remarkable person', my father said – although it was unclear whether this opacity was to protect the recovery of the patient or the commercial value of the treatment, or some useful blurring of the two. Again, all this made me uneasy, distrustful, but we did not push him for the details. After all, it was impossible to deny the change in him, the transformation, and we did not want to break whatever spell he might be under.

5

THERE ARE MANY DIFFERENT FORMS OF MENTAL
illness and each era has sought to categorise and understand
them in different ways. When Bethlem Hospital, special-
ising in the care and control of the insane, opened at its
new site in Moorgate in 1676 two sculpted male figures,
'Raving Madness' and 'Melancholy Madness', adorned its
front gates. A little larger than life-sized, classically muscu-
lar, naked except for loincloths, they represented the two
contemporary visions of madness: one wild, frenzied, struggling in its chains, the result of too much blood in the body;
the other morose, listless, withdrawn from the world, the
result, it was believed, of an excess of bile.

Over the centuries, the madhouses, bedlams, asylums
and mental and psychiatric hospitals housed a diverse and
changing demographic – including, at different times,
people with epilepsy, those with Down syndrome, the mentally handicapped and the morally compromised (whether
gay or wanton) – but were always most associated with
the more florid forms of mental illness, in particular what

is now diagnosed as schizophrenia: 'raving' rather than 'melancholy' madness. During this time melancholia, or depression, had been variously stigmatised – a sickness of the soul that was an insult to God, especially when it led to the mortal sin of suicide – and romanticised as evidence of profundity of thought or artistic genius. With the dawning of the asylum age, severely but non-psychotically depressed people, who would previously have been left, more or less, to their own devices, began to be institutionalised. They were subjected, at different times, to a range of treatments of varying uselessness and barbarity – prolonged baths, ECT without anaesthesia, lobotomy, zombifying medication – but in its idealised form, of course, the asylum was intended to provide a genuine and humane refuge from the cares, and quite possibly abuses, of ordinary life, a community in which the depressed might recover their sense of well-being. Samuel Tuke, grandson of moral-treatment pioneer William Tuke, described the approach at the York Retreat: 'In regard to melancholiacs, conversation on the subject of their despondency is found to be highly injudicious. The very opposite method is pursued. Every method is taken to seduce the mind from its favourite but unhappy musings, by bodily exercise, walks, conversation, reading, and other innocent recreations.'

Certainly, some people with depression experienced going into asylums and psychiatric hospitals as a relief. Anna Agnew, certified in 1878 and confined to the Indiana Hospital for the Insane, wrote later that, 'Before I had been an inmate of the asylum a week, I felt a greater contentment

than I had felt for a year previous. Not that I was recon-
ciled to life, but because my unhappy condition of mind
was understood, and I was treated accordingly. Besides, I
was surrounded by others in like bewildered, discontented
mental states in whose miseries… I found myself becoming
interested, my sympathies becoming aroused.' A patient at
Severalls described how the space and security helped her
recover from her illness: 'There was plenty of places to look
and come to terms with one's feelings… It was an asylum,
so that in the grounds, you know, you were safe. It was an
asylum, and yet you were free.'

It was strange to read my mother's abbreviated account of
her illness over a fifty-year period laid out in black and white,
a document written for researchers, entirely unsentimen-
tal, but full of intimate, sometimes devastating detail. She
wanted to give me the facts, I think, and it felt significant;
again, an acknowledgement of my own experience, that this
was something that connected us, or something that had
been unspoken too long. Perhaps it was easier than going
through it all again, or just a way to start. Parts of the story
were familiar to me and other parts were new, and I started
to rearrange my own memories around her account.

Once she had resigned from her job with the garden
designer, my mother withdrew, more or less completely, to
my parents' bedroom. It is hard to write about this time
from my own point of view, to give shape or substance or
coherence or conviction to it. Not only because it was a
long time ago and memories are vague or inaccessible, or

because it is upsetting, but because, with the exception of a handful of moments that remain vivid and definitive in my mind, it was a time when almost nothing seemed to happen. My mother lay in bed, hour after hour, day after day, month after month, sleeping or not sleeping, but certainly catatonic. The curtains were permanently drawn so the light was always dim in there, and the air was thick with the atmosphere of a room which was always occupied but not lived in. On my mother's bedside table were packets and bottles of pills, a glass of water to take them with, perhaps a glass of Complan, the food supplement she took because she was barely eating, and on the shelf below was a steadily accumulating pile of books that advertised the problem but which I never saw her read: *Self-Help for Your Nerves*, *Breakdown* (I can picture the jagged, fragmenting font of the title), *Depression*. Radio 4 played quietly and constantly, the low, unceasing murmur adding to the sense of some endless stasis or torpor. The landscape is featureless, dreary, each day the same as the one before and after it, no light or shadow, no texture. Perhaps that is the essential nature of acute depression, at least viewed from the outside, a flattening out, a terrible passivity, a void which nevertheless drags everything else towards it.

I cannot imagine what was in my mother's mind during this period and I am reluctant to try. As many people have observed, depression is a country the undepressed cannot enter. And yet it seems clear that although depression might present itself as an absence in the external, material, social, shared world, it is in fact a force turned brutally inward.

Perhaps her bed was the closest she could find to a refuge, where she felt least awful, or perhaps it was the opposite, the place where she was most able to devote herself to feeling bad. The physical catatonia of the depressed person is a response to, is perhaps in inverse relationship to, the intensity and intolerable drama of their interior world – guilt, shame, self-hatred, paranoia, the 'almost arterial agony' that the writer and psychologist Kay Redfield Jamison described in her own experience of depression.

What I felt about all this myself, in 1984, is not clear to me now. I was nine – the age my son is now – and could not have understood the strange force that took my mother out of her own life and out of ours. I cannot retrieve the feelings that sit beyond these flickering images and details. Nevertheless I felt – I must have felt – the presence of great difficulty and unhappiness, the sense of life going wrong, of things that were too difficult to talk about. I know that I have rarely talked about it, held it close, and that writing about it now feels uncomfortable, compelling.

If my overriding memory of this period is one of stasis and torpor, my brother – five years older and that much more aware – fills in other details, though, like me, he cannot always place them precisely in time. My mother's illness had taken on a highly paranoid, delusional edge. On the rare occasions when she did go out, she believed that people were crossing the road to avoid her or spitting at her as they went past. My brother remembers watching snooker on the TV with my parents and my mother being convinced the players were making gestures at her through the screen. These were some of the most distressing times, he says. She was adamant about these beliefs and could not be reasoned with. My parents had shouting rows, something that had never happened before. I do remember one occasion like this and it was certainly shocking. We were driving to London, to my mother's parents, no doubt to relieve some of the pressure on my father, when my mother became convinced that people were breaking into the house. She grabbed the wheel to make my father turn around. He lost his temper and pulled up the car. 'We're going home,' he shouted, as angry as I have ever seen him, 'and that will be the end of this fucking marriage.' I am pretty certain of these words. When we got back he came into the living room where my brother and I were watching TV. 'Don't worry about what I said,' he told us. 'We will always stay together.'

In my mother's document she wrote, 'My GP was supportive but I ended up in Severalls Hospital in summer 1984.' I was old enough, then, to know about Severalls, although I had never seen it – the madhouse somewhere out on the edge of town, near where I would soon be going to school, behind gates and walls, as obscure and mysterious, as dreaded and strange, as my mother's illness itself. But I did not know much more than this, then and for a long time after. Beyond the aborted attempt to take her out for the day, I do not remember the specifics of this time – the day my mother went into hospital or came out, or what it was like at home in the intervening period when she wasn't there, or what I was told about it all. We did not talk about any of this and despite this, or perhaps because it was implicit in our not talking about it, I somehow understood that my mother had been terribly unhappy in Severalls, one of the nadirs of her illness.

As it turned out, she was only a patient there for six weeks. No time at all, really, the length of a school summer holiday, the same length of time as my father. In her summary, Severalls warranted just four lines, fifty words out of 1,500. But my sense that she had suffered there was accurate. She did not find it a refuge. In her document she wrote that she was a very uncooperative patient and had received unsympathetic care, but did not go into detail, and I wondered what particular traumas or incidents her words might have elided. When we sat down to talk about it she elaborated a little. She didn't want to take part in occupational therapy, she told me, which included line dancing – perhaps this had replaced Barton's hula-hooping – and this annoyed the doctors and nurses. They prescribed Stelazine, an antipsychotic, which gave her lockjaw, and she refused more medication. At case conferences the doctors sat and discussed whether she was ready to go home. My father came to see her every day, and this must have felt like a strange return for him. My mother wandered the grounds, which were beautiful, and sat in quiet corners. Overall, what she felt in Severalls, she told me, was an intense feeling of loneliness.

Loneliness is a condition of depression, of course, but it is not hard to see how it would have been intolerably heightened by being in Severalls. It was a place full of strangers, doctors and nurses whom she did not trust, as well as other patients, many of them very unwell. As Russell Barton had written in *Institutional Neurosis,* admission to a psychiatric hospital involved a dissolution of your identity – the roles that orientate you – as a husband or wife, father or mother, son or daughter, friend, neighbour, employee. It cut you adrift from your own life, from everything that was familiar to you. It cut you off, too, as Andrew Solomon, author of *The Noonday Demon,* puts it, 'from the company of those who had any natural cause to love you'. I think of my own terror, when I was ill, of being sent away.

My mother remembers one middle-aged nurse who was more sympathetic. She told the nurse she felt like she was in a glass jar and the world was on the outside. Sylvia Plath used the same metaphor of confinement and isolation to describe the breakdown and depression of Esther Greenwood, her avatar in *The Bell Jar:* 'Wherever I sat – on the deck of a ship or at a street café in Paris or Bangkok – I would be sitting under the same glass bell jar, stewing in my own sour air.' My mother had not read *The Bell Jar.* Perhaps she had picked the idea up somewhere but it did not feel borrowed. Rather, it seemed like an example of the way that the experience of depression is both so particular and so generic that people gravitate towards the same language. The bell jar, as Plath suggests, follows you around, but I cannot help seeing many of its qualities – separation, confinement, isolation, claustrophobia – in the asylum itself, in Esther Greenwood's nameless private hospital, in McLean Hospital where Plath herself was treated, in the sequestered, semi-rural grounds of Severalls.

6

IN LATE 2011 OUR SECOND CHILD, A BOY, WAS BORN.
I was terrified about how I would cope – I had not coped
well the first time around – but he was an easy-going baby,
healthy, a good sleeper. My anxiety seemed to be under control. I had been writing again and one of my stories had
been shortlisted for a prize which came with a substantial
amount of money. The ceremony was being held at an
Oxford college and we booked rooms for ourselves as well
as my parents and parents-in-law. The grandparents would
look after the kids whilst Ellie and I went to the ceremony.
My father was well again and it felt like a celebration, regard-
less of whether or not I won the prize.

A few days before we were due to go to Oxford I began
to feel unwell. It seemed like a nasty flu and I lay in bed
taking aspirin and paracetamol every four hours, barely able
to eat, trying to keep my fluids up. The day before the trip
I still couldn't stand up and we made the decision to cancel.
By the time someone texted me from the ceremony to tell
me I hadn't won I felt too ill to care. I had developed a pain

in my right side that felt like a pulled muscle and getting to the bathroom and back exhausted me completely. The prize aside, I had picked another bad time to be ill. Our son was only six months old and our daughter was in her first year of school. Over the last few years I had been making a habit of not being much use, of dramatising my health. It felt like part of the usual pattern and Ellie was frustrated. But on the seventh night I began to feel even worse and I asked her to call an ambulance. In Accident and Emergency I asked the doctor if I was going to be OK. 'You're in the right place,' he said.

I was moved to a bed in intensive care and given an oxygen mask that strapped over my mouth and nose. They put me on fluid, painkiller and antibiotic drips, and took blood and sputum samples. An X-ray showed that both my lungs were black with infection and the tests confirmed the diagnosis of bacterial pneumonia. My lungs were failing and my blood was starved of oxygen. On my fourth day in hospital I was put into a medically induced coma but the antibiotics did not work and my condition did not stabilise. I was diagnosed with severe sepsis – a whole-body inflammatory state – and then, a few days later, acute respiratory distress syndrome (ARDS), the lungs' extreme reaction to an infection. The alveoli become inflamed, then collapse, the lungs harden and the oxygen saturation in the blood drops rapidly. Even if treated, ARDS has a fifty per cent mortality rate. The literature says: 'as loss of aeration progresses, the end tidal volume eventually grows to a level incompatible with life'.

I was kept in the coma for twenty-two days. A breathing

tube down my throat pumped 100 per cent oxygen into my lungs. An intravenous line in my neck delivered up to eight different drugs from bags that hung from metal stands next to the bed. Drugs to treat the infection, drugs for sedation and paralysis, drugs to keep my heart going despite the sedating and paralysing drugs, drugs to drain excess fluid. There was a feeding tube up my nose and down into my stomach, and saline and electrolyte drips into my arms. Every thirty minutes another line took blood out of my arm to be sent away for testing. I had a catheter in my penis, another in my anus, five sticky pads on my chest to monitor my heart and a clip, like a clothes peg, on my finger that shone an infrared light through my blood to measure the oxygen saturation.

After ten days the oxygen level in my blood had still not stabilised and I was moved to an oscillator, a machine that provided a different, more aggressive form of ventilation. The oscillator holds the brittle lungs open whilst air is pumped in and out, and the whole body vibrates with the force of it. A cooling blanket with freezing air pumped through it was laid over me to keep my raging temperature down. I was bloated with fluid, my whole body swollen up so that I was almost unrecognisable. These were, I was told later, the worst, the most dangerous days. There was a box on a trolley by the side of the bed with a sellotaped sign, 'Emergency Lung Drain Kit', which Ellie said looked alarmingly basic. The consultants discussed moving me to another London hospital where I could be given extracorporeal membrane oxygenation, in which blood is passed out of the body and through a machine that puts in oxygen and takes out carbon dioxide. It is the final throw of the dice. In the end, they decided it was too risky to move me.

There were family summits and conversations about what would happen after my death. Ellie checked the mortgage cover, my life insurance and my death-in-service payout from work. She wrote down a conversation with my father-in-law during which she said, of me, 'He's going, Dad.' They brought my five-year-old daughter in to see me. They explained it to me months later, when I went back for an outpatient appointment. 'If there is a loss,' the consultant said, 'research shows that children do better if they have had a chance to see the sick parent.' When she came in, my daughter patted the cooling blanket tentatively and called me 'pipe-man'. She was not visibly upset, but the next day, at school, she drew a picture and wrote underneath, 'I am sad Mummy.'

One of the consultants told Ellie and my brother that I was 'the sickest man in London right now, and maybe the whole country'. They both wrote this down. It was not, everyone agreed, a helpful thing to say – baseless and melodramatic. Surely there were people somewhere actually on the point of death, who in fact did die. I could not be sicker than them. But when, instead of dying, I got better, I liked the way it made me sound notorious – the Sickest Man in London – and I held on to it as a badge of honour.

After seventeen days in a coma things began to change. My oxygen levels stabilised, the infection retreated and I was moved from the oscillator back to a normal ventilator. On the twenty-third day they gave me a tracheostomy so that the breathing tube could be passed directly through my throat rather than my mouth. My brother remembers that as a good day, a sign of progress. Then they began to reduce the sedation. I am told that at first, when I woke up, I seemed happy and very high, but within a few hours I had become confused, paranoid. I asked my nurse, John, to show me his ID. I tried to rip out the lines on my arms. They put white cotton mittens like boxing gloves on my hands to stop me but still I thrashed at them and tried to fight the nurses with my puny, muscle-wasted arms and legs. I begged to see or speak to Ellie and demanded to be moved to another hospital where the staff were not trying to kill me.

Intensive care unit delirium or psychosis affects around a third of patients who stay longer than a few days in intensive care. It is caused by illness, medication, the withdrawing of medication, sleep deprivation, the distress of people in the other beds, the starkly lit, noisy, relentless and alien environment of the ward itself, or all of these things together. Massive doses of diamorphine had kept me in the coma and now I was coming off it.

The delusions were vivid and total. I was strapped into a dentist's chair in a seaside hotel. Around the room, a kind of bar or casino, there were others strapped into chairs. I did not want to be there but had come anyway, and I knew something was going to happen, something half thrilling, half terrible. The young, attractive woman who strapped me in and reclined the chair smiled and talked reassuringly to me, but I knew she was wicked. The room, with its flashing lights and red and white leather, had the gaudy, nightmarish feel of an amusement arcade, of twisted fun, of sexual pleasure and threat – and the chair was part of some hellish fairground ride. I wanted to leave but the woman was leaning over me, strapping me tighter, urging me to relax and submit. On the side of the chair was a lever with a red knob at the top, like the arm of a fruit machine. I was waiting for her to speak the words I seemed to fear but also long for, an offer with no possibility of refusal. 'Time for another suction, Tom?' she said, and then she would reach up and pull down the lever. Later, I would come to in the street, wrecked and wretched, and start trying to find my way back to the hotel.

In another sequence, the Face Project was a company contracted by the hospital to carry out cutting-edge therapeutic work with recovering patients. Their treatment centre, attached to the hospital, was bright and modern, and the staff were all young, hyper-cheerful and efficient, casually dressed in jeans, trainers and yellow Face Project T-shirts. The whole place – not to mention the name – projected the freshness and zeal of an internet start-up, or a cult. I was taken to a series of seminar rooms where patients were given iPads and seated in a circle. One of the T-shirted staff led us through a series of psychodynamic exercises that were designed to revive and sharpen our mental functioning, but which I did not understand and could not get the hang of. I asked the staff lots of questions – what exactly was the relationship between the Face Project and the hospital? When would I be going back to intensive care? – but they ignored them or changed the subject. They seemed distracted now, a little brusque. Eventually I was alone, lying on a bed in a small room where I could touch all four walls by stretching out my arms and legs. No one had been to see me for some time but I had no means of leaving. I noticed that the walls stopped about five feet from the floor and if I sat up in the bed I could see over them. What had impressed me as a sophisticated labyrinth of offices and high-tech treatment rooms was suddenly revealed as a few roughly partitioned cubicles within one drab and not very large space. All of the other cubicles were now abandoned.

'Sundowning' sounds benign – tranquil, poetic, a little druggy perhaps. In intensive care, however, it describes a pattern whereby patients suffering from delirium become more agitated at night, a kind of grim descent into greater fear and delusion. This seems to fit a metaphysical rather than medical logic – night-time is the time for spooks and ghosts, witches and demons, and for terror. Even in normal, everyday life, it is harder to stay sane in the middle of the night. I was told that one night during my own delirium, every time my nurse approached me or our eyes met, I mouthed – I could not speak – deadly serious, 'You're trying to kill me.' In the morning, just as she was finishing her shift, demoralised, I woke from a doze with no memory of the night. 'Hello,' I said, brightly, 'how are you?'

The psychosis passed after a few days and I began to recover. The tracheostomy still in place, I used a mangled sign language or mouthed the words I could not say out loud. I had a small whiteboard but my handwriting usually let me down. My brother said it was painful to watch me labouring over each letter, producing only minute, unrecognisable, runic figures. After a week or two the nurses started to lower the cuff in my throat so that I could speak and it was remarkable to hear my own voice. I started sitting for a few minutes each day in the chair beside my bed. Soon after that the tracheostomy was removed and I started eating small amounts of food and using a frame to take a few steps along the ward.

I was doing well – everyone said so. Each morning when the consultants came around they told me how much better I looked, what great progress I was making. Nurses I didn't know but who seemed to know me called out, 'Looking good today!' as they went past. I acknowledged the compliments, smiled and said, yes, I was feeling pretty good; I wanted to believe. I had become, or so I felt, a kind of celebrity patient. I was the erstwhile Sickest Man in London. I had come back from the dead, the void, the abyss. And now I was the longest-serving patient on the ward, an old hand, an intensive care veteran. I was enjoying myself. I had a kind of status.

I began to get visits from medical and nursing students who needed a case study for projects they were working on. There were several posh and polite young men, dressed in the uniform of aspiring consultants: pale chinos, brown leather shoes, shirts tucked in but tieless, and sensible hair. I imagined them rowing, or playing hockey. One medical student I had seen around the ward for a few days asked if she could talk to me about my 'experiences'. She drew the curtains around the bed, sat down and leaned in towards me. Her name was Sarah-Jane, she had a lot of freckles and her first question was, 'How does it feel to know you nearly died?' It was as well she had not been to see me whilst I was still delirious: she would have gone straight into my nightmares. Her question did not seem very medical, but it tapped into my vanity. I had been lying awake a lot at night and was in a philosophical mood. I said, 'You're very direct, aren't you?'

I cried a lot for myself, pure self-pity, which I felt I was entitled to, at least for a while. I thought of my daughter coming to see me, the psychologist asking her questions about how she felt. I was very tender; I could cry in an instant. But it was a sweet kind of sadness, like thinking about your own funeral and all the people who would come and be sad, and it was not so far from elation, elation that I had survived and was going to be OK. Before all this my mother-in-law had called me the Creaking Door because, she said, 'there is always something a little bit wrong with you but you will probably go on for ever'. I liked this because it was vivid and because it attributed to me a kind of strength and resolve, like an Indian chief – Sitting Bull, Standing Bear, Crazy Horse, Creaking Door. After seven weeks in intensive care I was moved into a general ward. Two weeks later I was discharged altogether.

7

I FELT DISAPPOINTED AT HOW LITTLE MY MOTHER remembered, or wanted to remember, about being in Severalls. Disappointed, too, at how short her stay had been, when it had occupied so much space in my mind. What had I hoped for? Hair-raising or sensational details of what life was like in a psychiatric hospital, I suppose. The same colour and detail of my father's account, perhaps, the eccentric patients, quack doctors and dubious treatments, but with a darker, harder edge. Details that would fill the gap and justify the taboo, the silence; some new and sharper insight into my mother's experience, the enigma of her illness.

Whatever the precise details of her stay there, it is clear Severalls did little or nothing for my mother's health. She was discharged and the following spring she took an overdose of the antidepressant Prothiaden. I do remember this. I had come home from school with a friend and there was a note on the table by the front door: 'Gone shopping, Love Mum.' I do not know if she had been shopping and come back or if the note was a deliberate deception to buy her time. We went up to my room but when my father came home from work sometime later he found her unconscious in their bedroom. I remember him shouting and slapping her face to bring her round, and then an ambulance arriving. I remember then lying on the front lawn as she was carried out to the ambulance, or perhaps after it had gone. It was a sunny day – but then it always seems to be sunny in these memories – and I went to the house of my mother's best friend across the road.

My brother confirms the weather. He had arrived home to find my father calling the ambulance. After it had gone, he remembers going next door to sit with his friend Oscar. Oscar's mother made them macaroni cheese, which my brother didn't eat. My mother's friend walked me around her garden and told me about some of the flowers and plants, which I suppose were starting to bloom or come into leaf. May is the peak month for suicides, I read recently.

On the way out of the village, the ambulance pulled over because they thought my mother's heart had stopped. I had read this in her summary but she told me again as we sat talking in the conservatory at home. She was matter-of-fact about it, as she was talking about all these things now, frank about the detail. I was old enough to hear it then, I suppose; entitled to hear it, even – I'm not sure. I had some sense of this seriousness at the time, I think – the drama of the discovery and the ambulance – but it shocked me to learn about it now, and whenever I think about it my own heart seems to stop for a moment, or perhaps I am just holding my breath; a moment when everything hung in the balance, when life – all our lives – nearly went one way rather than another. It was the kind of hard, stark detail I suppose I had wanted, although now I felt guilty at that impulse.

My brother has strong memories of the first night my mother was in hospital. He and my father watched a sci-fi film on TV and then slept in the same room. He doesn't remember what they said, if anything, but he felt they were both contemplating the future if my mother didn't survive. I must have been asleep in my own room. My mother was unconscious for two days and my father was warned there might be brain damage. When she came round, my mother found, again, that the doctors and nurses were not sympathetic. Attempting suicide was something to be ashamed of. My father and brother went to see her in hospital and I was at my mother's friend's house across the road when they came back. They were eating bags of chips and were in an upbeat mood; she was going to be OK. At some point in the days after this, as I was walking out of the school gates, someone in my class asked me if my mother had tried to kill herself. I don't know how he knew, perhaps everyone did. 'She hasn't been very well,' I told him. 'They think it might have been an accident.' It is striking how clearly I remember these words. This was what I had been told, I suppose, that perhaps she hadn't meant to overdose but had somehow taken the wrong medication or too much of it. I can't say now whether I really believed it.

A few months later, my mother took another overdose, this time of paracetamol. Neither my brother nor I was aware of this second attempt at the time but my father decided he couldn't cope with her at home. She refused to go back to Severalls and through a friend of my grandfather's, a professor at the Royal Free Hospital in London, she was admitted to a psychiatric ward there. It was the most amazing dump of a place, my mother told me. It stank of urine and there was one lounge there, with a television, a table tennis table and not much else – but at least it was not Severalls. The staff were kinder and the regime less strict. My mother played table tennis and went to relaxation classes. There was art therapy, too, though she was scornful of this, as she had been of the occupational therapy at Severalls.

The Royal Free is a general hospital, not a psychiatric hospital, so the feel was different, and the patients were different, too. Most of them had eating disorders, my mother recalls, and one was being guarded by two officers from Holloway prison. One night the woman stole my mother's clothes and escaped, before being picked up in Plymouth a few days later. For several weeks after my mother was admitted nothing seemed to happen. There were none of the case conferences she had been used to at Severalls and she had to beg to see a psychiatrist. Eventually she was prescribed Mellaril, another antipsychotic, and, without consultation with my father, given a course of ECT. My father was outraged when he found out, but admitted later that my mother had seemed to improve a little afterwards. As Esther Greenwood says, following a session of ECT, 'The bell jar hung, suspended, a few feet above my head. I was open to the circulating air.'

My mother stayed at the Royal Free for several months and my brother and I spent some of that summer with my grandparents in London. My brother remembers that my father had started making goulash stews and we would eat these together on Sundays. Again, I only remember visiting my mother once during this time. Again, it was sunny and we took her out for a picnic on Hampstead Heath. My mother was cheerful, or seemed to be, and my father and brother – both nuts about politics – were excited because we saw Michael Foot, who had been the leader of the Labour Party until the election defeat two years before, walking his dog slowly up the street. It was the day of Live Aid, 13 July 1985, and we listened on the car radio on the way to London and back again. My mother remembers it as the year Boris Becker first won Wimbledon. We had always watched tennis together as a family, a summer ritual, but this time she watched it alone on the TV in the hospital lounge.

PART FOUR

A memory that does not leave my heart

I

IN 1994 SEVERALLS WAS FINALLY SLATED FOR closure. Over the previous decade the number of patients had shrunk from around 1,000 to 500. Wards had been closed, starting with the most out of date, the most isolated and those on the upper floors of the buildings. When staff left they weren't replaced or people on only temporary contracts were employed. The hospital had been absorbed into the community mental health team and the policy of de-institutionalisation and decentralisation had begun to accelerate. The last patient left on 20 March 1997.

All across the country the old asylums were closing in their droves. After thirty years of confusion, neglect and gradual decline, the impetus of Thatcherite cost-cutting and managerialism was now swiftly realising the vision of Enoch Powell's water-tower speech. By the turn of the century nearly all of them would be shut. In and around London alone, the 1990s saw the closure of Bexley (originally the Heath Asylum) in Dartford; Friern (the Middlesex County Pauper Lunatic Asylum) in Barnet; Cane Hill (the

Third Surrey County Pauper Lunatic Asylum) in Coulsdon; Caterham Mental Hospital (the Metropolitan Imbecile Asylum); Claybury (the Fifth London County Council Pauper Lunatic Asylum) in Redbridge; Horton Asylum (the Seventh London County Council Asylum), Long Grove Hospital (Long Grove Asylum) and Manor Hospital (the Sixth London County Council Asylum) in Epsom; Normansfield Hospital in Kingston; Royal Earlswood (Earlswood Asylum for Idiots) in Redhill; and Tooting Bec Mental Hospital (Tooting Bec Asylum). It was a revolution or, more accurately, a counter-revolution. These often huge institutions had spread in a vast network across the physical, social and cultural landscape of the country. Now they were gone, leaving behind a legacy of dereliction, demolition and redevelopment.

The closure of Severalls appears to have gone unmourned, at least in public. I trawled the archive of the local paper in this period. There is the usual combination of news stories: endless arguments about town-centre parking, children suspended from school for inappropriate haircuts, a streaker in Castle Park, the arrival of new animals at the zoo, a series of big-cat and UFO sightings, fights after pub closing time on Friday and Saturday nights, occasionally a murder. There is a six-page souvenir supplement celebrating Colchester's 'special relationship' with the recently dead Princess Diana. There are almost weekly stories about a beds crisis at the General Hospital and the possibility of new cuts or funding, but I could find no mention at all of Severalls. It felt like a conspiracy of silence, that in some essential way the hospital remained taboo even now, a source of shame and stigma, but the truth is probably more prosaic. By this time, the place was already half forgotten, old news.

After 1997 a small section of the site was retained by the Trust, which continued to run some administrative and inpatient services from one of the old villas, as well as coordinating the other mental health services that now existed in forty-five different locations across the north of the county. The medical superintendent's former house was turned into a long-stay unit for half a dozen patients, and a small secure unit also remained. For the next twenty years the Trust, the council and potential developers wrangled over the sale and redevelopment of the site. The local and even, from time to time, national newspapers did keep track of this saga. Initial plans, submitted in 1999, which proposed retaining the old dance hall and the central playing fields amongst other existing hospital buildings, fell through despite seemingly general approval. In 2001, a Save Severalls Campaign began to resist new plans for the redevelopment because of the amount and type of new housing, pressures on local infrastructure and the volume of traffic. At this time, it was reported that Colchester's housing boom meant it was running out of new postcodes.

The Save Severalls Campaign and others accused the Trust of failing to properly secure the site and the hospital buildings and that, as a result, it had gone 'from being one of the best preserved of its type to being in a state of severe disrepair'. In 2008 the slump in the housing market caused more redevelopment plans to collapse. In 2010 a group of travellers were reported to have broken in and set up camp, and around the same time a petition was got up to oppose the latest development proposals. Campaigners had some minor successes. The hospital chapel was demolished but the organ and stained-glass windows were saved. The windows, commissioned in 1963 for the hospital's golden anniversary, showed Jesus in the centre with a nurse, doctor and patients on their knees looking up at him. The organ was shipped to France and reinstalled in a church in Brittany. In November 2013, ex-patients and staff were invited on a farewell tour of the hospital, where they wrote on a commemorative wall which, according to the local paper, would be 'photographed and preserved', a rather muted bookend to the open days of 1913 when the new institution threw open its doors for inspection by the public. There are photos of the wall in the paper, but I have not been able to find out what became of it afterwards.

The Severalls site was not alone in its painful and protracted transition to the post-asylum age. There were similar stories all around the country. Subject to economic ups and downs, disputes between developers and planners, or – as conservationists often suspected – a conspiracy to run them into the ground, it is tempting to see the persistence of the asylums in their material form as somehow symbolic, ghosts in the landscape, the social fabric and the private and public imagination. 'Do not for a moment underestimate their powers of resistance to our assault,' said Powell in 1961. Now, the 150-year-old idea was dead, but no one had yet imagined what the future would look like without it.

*

The asylums may have disappeared but the patients could not simply be disappeared with them. At least, not literally. De-institutionalisation was often brutal. Beginning in the 1960s, 100,000 long-stay patients were decanted out of UK psychiatric hospitals – back to family, into supported housing, to psychiatric wards in general hospitals and to a patchwork of other vastly inadequate services – a policy already widely regarded as a disaster by the 1990s. 'Care in the community' became a synonym for the troubled, isolated or simply odd, and passed into the language as a general insult. The radical optimism of Marco Cavallo's march out of San Giovanni asylum and into the streets of Trieste was a distant dream.

Many former long-stay patients simply became part of the new and large population of 'revolving door' patients, people who were admitted repeatedly for short periods. Barbara Taylor, herself part of the revolving door at Friern Hospital, wrote of her own panic when closure was announced. 'So what will happen when the hospital closes down?' she asked her friend Magda. 'We'll hide out, and when everybody else has gone we'll take it over.' Despite the changes there were still some long-stay patients in the asylums right up until the end, and the fate of these people, often the most vulnerable, has a particular pathos. At Severalls, in 1997 there were people who had been resident there for sixty years. One woman wrote to institutions all over the country asking if they would give her a bed once she was forced to leave. The outcome of her request is not recorded.

The chief executive of North East Essex Mental Health

NHS Trust was tasked with running down and closing Severalls. His background was as an executive at the BBC and Rolls Royce, and in an interview in 1997 he spoke of it as a managerial conundrum, as well as potentially a PR problem. He noted that amongst the elderly patients who were moved into nursing homes there was a 'horrific' spike in the death rate. He pointed out that 'these were long-stay patients who might have died anyway', though this does not seem to account for the spike. He admitted concern about the possibility of former inpatients slipping through the net of other support services and where they might end up. 'We did more than anyone else to get the homeless shelter started in Colchester,' he said, apparently without irony. The homelessness was a failure 'not of this service, that's a failure of the whole system... I guess there is a group of people who don't want to be helped, for whom we probably don't provide much help.' Asked if, overall, he felt positive about what had happened during these years, he interrupted the interviewer: 'Yes. Proud is the word you are looking for.'

Initial projects designed to monitor the impact of de-institutionalisation on patients in certain parts of the country reported back optimistically, but they were limited in scope and duration and driven by a particular agenda. In general, having managed patients out of the hospital system, little attempt was made to log, track and analyse their future movements or fate. Some patients found better lives outside the old asylums but for others it meant new and often more desperate problems – a drift from day care to hostels to acute wards on general hospitals to homelessness to prison, a new rootlessness. Those who did not engage with the system, who in the words of the chief executive in charge of Severalls 'don't want to be helped', could not be counted at all. In this sense they had, after all, been made to disappear.

2

THE EXPERIENCE OF INTENSIVE CARE OFTEN LEAVES long-term psychological scars, even on people who have spent a short time there, and is sometimes diagnosed as post-traumatic stress disorder. Ellie and my brother were aware of this possibility. They joked to each other – they told me later – that given my history and my marathon stay in intensive care, as soon as I was well enough to be discharged they would escort me straight across the road to the Maudsley, the UK's largest remaining psychiatric hospital. This was not unreasonable. Once I was out of the coma, one of my first questions was about venlafaxine, the antidepressant medication I was taking before I went into hospital. The doctors reassured me they had been giving this to me intravenously whilst I was sedated, but now I was awake I was conscious of having no access to the Ativan I occasionally still relied on for managing my anxiety. If I had been worried about my health before I'd been in intensive care, it was certainly plausible that I would be more so in the future. What might such a dramatic shock to my physical system do to my shaky mental well-being?

I did not end up in the Maudsley, or anywhere else. In the immediate aftermath of being in hospital, in fact, I was on a high. Death gives meaning to life, no doubt, and life now felt deeply meaningful – how could it not? People came to visit me at home whilst I was convalescing – and later, when I was stronger, took me out to lunch – and I told the story over and over, enjoying the extremity and rarity of my experience, its life-affirming arc. At the follow-up appointment the consultant told me they had not expected me to make it, that my recovery was miraculous. After a few months of rest and physiotherapy I was back to full strength and had returned to work. This confirmed the narrative of remarkable resilience, to the Sickest Man in London and back. I had defied the odds – not just death but the possibility of oxygen tanks and permanent disability. It was more than full health, even. One friend suggested that I was ten per cent better than I was before I was ill, meaning it in the most general sense, a better person. He was not entirely serious but there was some truth in it, I think. I was a little bit reborn. Grateful for the kindness and care I had received, grateful to be alive. In the few months after getting out of hospital I fixed the central heating, took the U-bend off a sink and unblocked it, and changed a flat tyre on the car, all tasks previously beyond me. Ellie suggested that the doctors and nurses had rewired me when I was in the coma. I am reminded of the debunked psychiatric treatments of the past – neurotic or disturbed patients who were said to have awoken from insulin-, barbiturate- or opiate-induced comas rejuvenated and free of symptoms.

The high of recovery passed gradually but my overall mental health remained stable. From time to time I had brief but intense flashbacks of intensive care, impressions of being on the ward; a smell or an image or just a mood, some vivid sensory or emotional flavour that couldn't be translated into language. Over time I began to notice a pattern to these – they came in spring, within a few days of the anniversary of my hospital admission. They were not traumatic in the way you might imagine.

For me, this experience of profound physical illness was oddly therapeutic. The knowledge of what my body had been able to survive was potent, I think, a weapon against the nagging anxieties of physical ill health that I had lived with for a long time: the Creaking Door. Perhaps it is a mistake to generalise, but the way we experience and make sense of physical illness is different from that of psychological distress, even if the distinctions are often blurred. It seemed possible – in fact, accurate – to think of the illness that put me in intensive care as something separate from me. After all, I had caught it; the bacteria that caused the pneumonia had come from somewhere else. It did not matter that by most measures my physical illness had been far more serious than my anxiety, that it had very nearly killed me. We have ways of talking about it that make it knowable and understandable, a vocabulary of alveoli and inflammation and oxygen saturation that described in hard scientific terms what was happening to my body and treatments that could eradicate it. I had sometimes conceived of anxiety as an invader, too, but I had not caught it from somewhere else, at least not in any measurable way. In reality, it was a part of me. It had come from within and I had to think of myself differently after my breakdown, fundamentally so. This is something to do with the self, how we divide mind and body, but whilst an infection can be cured – modern medicine has seen to that – mental health is only ever provisional, conditional, subject to reversal.

My physical illness was different in other ways, too. Pneumonia felt like a public experience, or at least one with a strong manifestation in the external, material world – the rush to hospital in an ambulance, admission to intensive care, ventilation, sedation, a tracheostomy, discharge. Vast resources and expertise were expended on my care. There was a clear narrative, validated by concrete events, a story that I and others could tell in narrowly objective terms without the need for brooding interior reflection. My surprising and rapid recovery was measurable, quantifiable and celebrated.

But even whilst I was telling this story of unlikely triumph I knew that the life-affirming arc was only possible because of the specific circumstances of my illness: limited in duration (during the worst of which I was sedated and unaware) and with no long-term complications. At a meeting for former intensive care patients months later, I met others who had not been so fortunate – one with an oxygen tank; another, my age, who walked with a stick. I also knew that my family – whose experience of my illness was very different from my own – would not have described this time as therapeutic. There may have been complacency and hubris in how I was feeling. I knew by now that psychological impacts do not always show their hand immediately but play out over the long term.

3

IF THE OFFICIAL RECORD IS QUIET ON SEVERALLS IN the post-asylum period, the urge to memorialise the hospital has found expression elsewhere. I think again of the pictures taken by the urban explorers. The images of trashed wards and offices, piles of rubble and broken glass, the twisted relics of furniture and clinical equipment, graffitied walls. It seems surprising that this site, these buildings, these contents, were not cleared out, salvaged, properly shut down, carefully processed into some new future but instead left to decay, to be looted and vandalised. Worse, perhaps, the pictures show filing cabinets pulled over and paperwork spread across desks and floors – patient medical files according to some accounts: bureaucratic abandonment and chaos. All this feels symbolic, significant. The explorers had accessed the site illegally but had still taken the time to record everything they saw and found, out of the sense of obligation to the patients who had once lived there, their former home deserving of 'enormous attention and respect'.

There are two groups on Facebook dedicated to Severalls.

One is public and most of the contributors are urban explorers discussing trips to the site before the redevelopment. Some are serious about the history of the hospital and others more interested in the thrill of trespass and rumours of the paranormal. Over time, as the redevelopment plans gain pace, entry becomes more difficult. A number of them make plans for one last trip on Halloween. They post shakily shot videos that track down the corridors and, like a found horror movie, something awful seems about to happen. Some claim to have had ghostly experiences. One describes being in the old kitchens late on a summer evening when, 'for a split second around the outside there were Mummies... like ppl wrapped in bed sheets from head to toe must of been about 11 or 12 scattered around... I heard footsteps in the corridors too.' Someone replies, 'I hope you can let the image go... and we can only pray that the souls go to rest... best to leave that alone. The troubles of this world are enough to contend with. I would not dabble in such things.' There is another reply, from someone who says they had been a patient at Severalls: 'You didn't visit when I was there in real time?!!! No ghosts just a hollow shell. Would you have the balls to face the insane doctors and nurses who experiment for laughs.' The original poster is not put off. 'Yes,' he writes back, 'nothing scares me.'

The other group is private and seems to fulfil a different need. It was set up in 2016 by two student documentary makers who had plans to make a film about the history of the hospital, and a teaser for the film can still be viewed online. They had been given authorised access and the site is shown as it was then, at the peak of its dereliction. Professionally shot and edited and set to an eerie orchestral score, the camera again tracks slowly down the long graffiti-daubed corridors and through ruined rooms thick with shadow, cutting to lingering close-ups of peeling wallpaper, piles of rubble and broken locks. 'Take a look behind closed doors,' the overlaid text reads, 'Discover the history', before a final drone shot zooms out to reveal the site from the air and the title appears: 'Secrets of Severalls – Coming Soon'.

For the first year or so the group is very lively. People are excited about the film and the group admins post periodic updates about its progress. The majority of the contributors to the group are former staff, their children, or nurses who trained there, many of them now retired, and the dominant mood is one of nostalgia – for the community, old colleagues and working life, for the grounds and buildings now being erased or about to be, for an era that has passed. There is talk of 'Dear old Sevs' and they post photos of themselves as they were then, in nursing uniforms, as members of the football and cricket teams, or taking part in an 'It's a Knockout' competition for staff and patients. They reconnect with old friends and reminisce about nights in the dance hall and the on-site social club, the cheap beer and the baked potatoes served up by the barman. One woman recalls how, on the night she qualified as a nurse, she and a friend rode a moped down the hospital corridors whilst drinking from a bottle of champagne.

There is anger, too, towards the Trust and its managers who dismantled and then closed the hospital, and the planners and developers who allowed it to fall into ruin before setting about its demolition. There is suspicion that the long delays were a deliberate plan to let some of the listed architecture degrade to the point where it would have to be demolished rather than converted, freeing the developers to eradicate the material legacy of the hospital entirely. There are conspiracy theories about the fire that destroyed the dance hall, too. As the demolition begins, people post photos of the building site tagged with weeping emoticons.

Occasionally, someone else, an urban explorer or ghost hunter, will ask a question about the darker or more complicated aspects of the hospital's history and myth, but this is given short shrift. 'When I worked there it was a hospital not a death camp,' replies one man. He goes on to joke that the only experiments he was aware of were carried out on the brains of the managers, 'turning them into mantra jabbering zombies with no foresight, talent or financial acumen'. From time to time someone mentions the particular atmosphere of the place – 'such sadness amongst such beautiful surroundings' – or alludes to the reputation for neglect or abuse, but even these posts are fiercely defensive of Severalls, and the asylum system itself: 'Severalls had many faults but are the mentally ill any better off without it?'; 'We closed them whilst Scandinavia rebuilt them!'; 'A haven and a home to so many'; 'Yes some people had bad memories but others owe their lives to the people there.'

The voices of former patients themselves are – perhaps not surprisingly – much rarer. The few there seem to have only been in Severalls for a brief period and do not offer much detail. According to one woman, who was an inpatient as a teenager, all the staff were lovely except one doctor who 'did nothing except ask me questions about sex which really had fuck all to do with why I had a breakdown'. Lunchtimes were grim, she says, 'always some bloke wanking under the table 😒'. There are, however, many people in the group who are relatives of former patients. They ask for information or memories of family they heard about but never met. One asks about his grandfather, a patient in Severalls from 1944 to 1962 following three years in a German prisoner-of-war camp. Another asks if anyone remembers her great-uncle who died in the hospital in 1959. No one in the family had ever mentioned him and now those that would remember were dead themselves.

A few recall their own parents' time at Severalls. One woman describes visiting her father at the hospital when she was a child. 'All I did know was that my Dad could not leave and go home with us,' she writes. 'One time when we were leaving the hospital my Dad told my Mum to ask the Doctor when he could go home with us. Dad's face changed from hopeful to hopeless when the Doctor said, "We'll see, we'll see." Then turned his back and walked away. That was so sad and a memory that does not leave my heart.' Several of these people compare notes about their own mental health struggles. One woman, who is diagnosed as bipolar and had spent time on psychiatric wards herself, describes how her mother was admitted to Severalls with post-natal depression. The family visited every weekend for four years until her mother came home. A later post shows a photo of a brick on a table. 'Just been to Severalls today as I wanted a little memento,' she writes. 'I called through the fence to a builder who kindly chose me this nice Red Brick as I'd asked. Going to get my Mum's name engraved in it.'

After a year, posts to the group begin to dry up. Someone asks when the film will be out and one of the documentary makers admits that there have been problems. They haven't been able to find funding, and interviewees have been reluctant to speak about their experiences on camera. Contributors to the group are disappointed and some are angry. In a subsequent post the documentary maker says that instead of a feature-length documentary, they will post an article on their website, which will include all the footage and materials they have gathered, but this too never appears.

4

THE SEVEN WEEKS I SPENT IN INTENSIVE CARE IS THE longest time I have ever been in hospital and although I experienced psychosis whilst I was there, it was as a limited side effect of a physical illness, not the cause of my admission. Overall, my experience of the mental health system has been an essentially modern one. When I had my breakdown I did not have any hospital treatment, let alone as an inpatient. In fact, I got little professional help of any kind – some pills that didn't work, then some that might have, a bit of counselling, a meeting with a psychiatrist. This is about what most people suffering from mild mental illness in this country can currently expect, if they are lucky. Most will probably never get as far as the psychiatrist. I self-medicated with Ativan the way many do with other drugs or alcohol. We are all vulnerable to the times we live in and I am glad I was not sucked into an over-zealous, institutional psychiatric system, heavily medicated, exposed to quack treatments like my father, forced to pass through the gates of the mad with who knows what implications for my sense of myself. And yet, it would have helped to have been prescribed the pills that gave me relief and offered better counselling or therapy. It sometimes seems as if, despite the advances in medication, 2,000 years has not got us much closer to solving or even managing the problem of mental illness.

I was lucky – and it feels like nothing more complex than luck – broadly speaking and in various ways. Many others are not so lucky. Their mental health is not so manageable and the support they need is very often not available. These are the people most likely to feel the radical change in how society has attempted to care for those with mental illness and least likely to benefit from the new narrative that encourages us all to speak more openly about our mental wellbeing. The closure of the asylums decimated the number of beds available for psychiatric care, placing an intolerable burden on general hospitals, community mental health teams and, very often, the families of those who are ill. Since the Health and Social Care Act 2012 governments have talked about giving equal priority to mental and physical health, but so far this has been a fantasy. Decades of underfunding have been compounded by the savage cuts of austerity. In the years 2011–2019 mental health trusts in England had real-term budget cuts of over eight per cent year on year. In the same period a third of all NHS mental health beds and fifteen per cent of mental health nurse jobs were lost. The adult psychiatric system is now run on a crisis model, where only the very sickest make it into hospital, usually under section. There they are medicated before being hustled rapidly back out into the community to make way for the next acutely ill patient. There is a high turnover of staff, little opportunity to build personal relationships and no capacity for preventative work. The pressures of the pandemic and the cost-of-living crisis have made the demand for services even higher. Of course, those that can afford to pay can still admit themselves to a private psychiatric hospital, as they have been able to since long before the creation of the public asylums.

This is not to say that sufferers would be better off consigned long term to a psychiatric institution or subjected to some of the grotesque treatments that took place in them. Some function well in the community and benefit from the independence and autonomy it gives them. But for many others the community is a very challenging place. The support services are not only thin on the ground, subjected to ever more cuts, but fragmented in a way that can make them difficult to navigate and access – supported housing, hostels, day centres and clinics. One of the principles of community care was to avoid a culture of dependency but the trade-off is lives of great insecurity, the high possibility of falling through the gaps. The stigma of the asylum is replaced by the stigma of the unhinged or dangerous lunatic running amok in the community. Asylums remain a polarising subject but it is not simple. Barbara Taylor wonders what would have happened to her if she had become ill now, instead of during the asylum age, without the refuge of Friern, her 'stone mother'. 'Would I make it?' she asks.

Not all the old asylums have gone or been converted or redeveloped. A short train journey and then a bus from where I live in south-east London took me to Bethlem Royal Hospital. Bethlem is the most iconic and enduring of mental health institutions, Europe's first psychiatric hospital, a continual and fraught symbol of morphing attitudes and policy over hundreds of years. Founded in 1247 as a priory in Bishopsgate in the City of London, in 1676, following the Great Fire of London, it moved to the site at Moorgate. The new hospital was a prestige building and a symbol of the rebuilt London's modernity and grandeur: vast, ornate, bearing a facade modelled on Louis XIV's Tuileries Palace and an octagonal turret with a cupola, surrounded by formal gardens and tree-lined promenades. The treatment of the mentally ill for the first time – but not for the last – became an emblem of social progress and civic aspiration.

The building was not all it seemed, however. It had no foundations and the weight of the elaborate facade caused the whole edifice to bow. The walls cracked and ran with water and, in what became a standard refrain of critics of mental health policy and radical theorisers, one observer wondered 'whether the persons that ordered the building of it, or those that inhabit it, were the maddest'. The conditions on the inside were dire – brutal, neglectful, humiliating – and it gained a grim reputation, not least through the spectacle of public visits. The word 'bedlam' entered the language as a synonym for malign chaos and confusion. In 1817 the hospital moved to another site, New Bethlem Hospital at St George's Fields in Southwark. The building was austere, utilitarian, stripped of the adornment and pretension that had attracted so much mockery and ire. The statues, Raving Madness and Melancholy Madness, that had adorned the gates at Moorgate, were placed more discreetly in the entrance hall, behind curtains. The central part of the building still remains, now the home of the Imperial War Museum, though the hospital moved nearly a century ago.

The Bethlem Royal Hospital, the current incarnation, opened in 1930 in Bromley amongst the apple orchards of Kent. Now part of South London and Maudsley NHS Foundation Trust, it has, remarkably and despite the controversial brand, survived the forces that have swept away so many other similar institutions. It continues to run residential and outpatient psychiatric services and represents something like the best that public mental health care currently has to offer – a mixture of services for a wide spectrum of patients, distributed amongst the villas and expansive parkland of the estate but also integrated into the community – a version of what progressive psychiatric reformers had always imagined. Whereas psychiatric wards and services are usually now an add-on to general hospitals, situated 'out of sight, round the back somewhere near the morgue', as a friend of mine, an NHS psychiatrist put it, the Bethlem site is unashamedly dedicated to them. The same friend, who worked at the National Psychosis Unit and mother and baby unit at Bethlem early in her career, remembers it as a unique and nearly ideal environment. But it is an outlier, an exception, its services in demand from patients across the country, able to treat only a fraction of those who need it.

The first thing I saw when I got off the bus outside the hospital gates was a sign that read 'No Photography'. Other

than that, however – and to my surprise – there was no pro-
hibition on my entering. I took a path that headed through
a copse of oak trees. At 270 acres the Royal Bethlem is close
in size to the old Severalls estate and gives a strong sense of
how that hospital might have appeared in the years before
its closure. Royal Bethlem was conceived and built seventeen years later than Severalls, with the same architectural
and philosophical principles in mind: a semi-rural location
of green space, air and light, a central administrative building complemented by the villa system, the monolithism and
homogeneity of the hospital at St George's Fields replaced
by different wards and departments around the grounds.

I passed the chapel, a pretty, good-sized building shaded
by long-established plane trees, like an upmarket village hall.
Beyond that was the water tower, now converted to the
estates and planning office, the rooftop crowded with mobile
phone and television masts. I went on. Huge, recently
mown lawns and sports fields were connected by pleasantly
wooded paths to the different wards and departments, and
I thought of 1960s university campuses, of Essex, where my
parents had worked, and UEA, where I had been a student.
There was Monks Orchard House, an autism assessment
and behavioural genetics clinic, and Tyson House, which
includes an adolescent psychiatric unit and an adult eating
disorders unit. There were newer buildings, too, but the
original structures were well maintained, the red brickwork
and stone cladding clean, the window frames bright white,
apparently in good repair. I passed an occupational therapy
garden, a swimming pool, a walled garden. At the far end

of the site, across more lawns, was a rare piece of dereliction – a bent metal sign on a rusting fence that stated 'Patients Only: Tennis Shoes Must Be Worn' and behind the fence the outline of an overgrown court. Amid all the havoc of mental illness it was somehow pleasing to see this injunction to wear the right shoes. There were other more modern and functioning tennis courts elsewhere on the site.

Towards the end of my circuit I passed a low-rise, modern building, with its own small garden enclosed by a ten-foot-high green mesh fence topped with large floodlights. 'Chelsham House', the sign said, described on the Trust's website as a unit for over sixty-fives with acute mental illness or under sixty-fives with dementia. Beyond this was a larger, many-storeyed, more forbidding building. Here the fence around the gardens was much higher, perhaps twenty feet, and at the top it curled back on itself, causing extra difficulty for anyone attempting to climb it from the inside. This was River House, a medium-security forensic unit.

Despite this evidence of confinement, perhaps of risk, of the more extreme and disturbed behaviours, the overwhelming impression to a visitor was one of tranquillity and space. It was a bright and unusually mild autumn day and red and gold leaves lay in drifts across the vast lawns. An elderly woman, a member of the public it seemed, was throwing a ball for her dog. It was all a far cry from the horrors of Bedlam or even the Severalls of my imagination. I thought of the old Severalls site, the new builds spreading rapidly across it, and wondered what might have been done differently.

A century ago, Royal Bethlem would have felt sequestered, remote, but now that the apple orchards are gone,
replaced by London residential sprawl, the gates open to
the public, the world inside the hospital seems continuous
with the world beyond it. Undoubtedly, the line between
the mentally well and the unwell, the sane and the insane,
has dissolved a great deal since the height of the asylum era.
Mental illness is no longer the preserve of people who are
not us. Mental health is provisional, for all of us. It has been
democratised and, as a result, a certain sort of stigma has
gone. It is not, quite, the dreadful, shameful secret it once
was. The existence of a four-part Channel 4 documentary
– 'Bedlam' – filmed inside the wards of Bethlem and other
parts of the Trust in 2013 seems illustrative of this. The films
focus on the patients and document their lives in intimate,
sometimes distressing, often very moving detail. The series
does not address the wider crisis in mental health provision
but acts as a reminder that, despite the strains, psychiatric
services continue to do good work and make a difference to
people's lives.

Circling back round to the front of the site I came to the
main building of the original design, the governor's block,
with its impressive facade, copper-green clock tower and circular driveway. Previously the centre of power at Bethlem,
from where all diagnosis, certification and treatment was
directed, it has been repurposed as Bethlem Museum of the
Mind. A free-to-enter public collection, the museum includes
artefacts of hundreds of years of mental health history –
straitjackets of different eras (one with a fashionably ruffled

collar), a section of padded wall, an anti-masturbation device that enclosed the penis in metal, an electronic tag of the type that patients of the secure units are now required to wear if they leave their ward, and an evolving display of artwork by present and former patients. On plinths in the foyer of the museum are the original statues of Raving Madness and Melancholy Madness that first adorned the gates of Bethlem in Moorgate before being concealed behind curtains at the new site in St George's Fields. I stood and marvelled at them – their size, the drama of their imagery, this fetishisation of suffering – and wondered how they had ever seemed like a good idea.

PART FIVE

The bullet

I

INTENSIVE CARE GAVE ME, FOR A WHILE, A SENSE OF being reborn but it had not cured me of anxiety. I continued to take Ativan occasionally. There were periods of weeks when I did not feel well, though never such that I could not go to work or carry on normal life. The anxiety was subject to no particular triggers that I could identify – not work, not money, not family, although all those could be stressful. Instead, as ever, the feeling was subject to its own mysterious cycles and rhythms. At these times, I slept badly and woke early, I had headaches, I was irritable, my appetite went, my energy was low and my concentration poor – but it was manageable. If it felt too much or I needed a good night's sleep, I took a pill. I stopped worrying about this. It felt a reasonable and efficient way of taking the edge off things until the moment passed. I always made sure to have a small supply and to restock from Chris when it ran low. I kept a single pill in my wallet, a kind of insurance policy, and from time to time I checked for it with my finger. A 'safety behaviour', therapists call this, disapprovingly.

When I went away, I took more, in my washbag, and checked several times before leaving to make sure they were there.

It was hard now, a few years on, to understand why I had been so neurotic about these pills. It is always difficult to relate to any state of mind you are not currently in – to imagine being sad when you are happy, happy when you are sad – and this is particularly true of illness, I think. When you are ill you cannot imagine being well and can only remember the other times you were ill. It feels as if you have always been ill. When you are well, illness seems like another life, or Virginia Woolf's 'undiscovered countries'. Perhaps there is some kind of psychological defence mechanism at work here, such as the way, I read somewhere, that the memory of the pain of childbirth is blunted so that a woman is not put off ever going through it again. By any stretch, my fears of benzodiazepine dependency and addiction had proved to be ludicrously overblown. The amounts I was taking were tiny – a normal prescription might be a daily dose two or three times larger – but I was in a state of high and relentless anxiety and not able to make reasonable judgements.

Andrew Solomon has argued that the fear of addiction has led to 'gross underuse of the benzos', that they are miraculous for the short-term treatment of anxiety and only a risk to people with a long-term history of substance abuse. Solomon was describing the situation in the US, where benzodiazepines are much more widely prescribed than they are in UK. 'I have met people,' he writes, 'who were tortured with psychic anguish that could have been alleviated had their physicians been more permissive in the prescription of the benzos'. I find it hard to disagree. During the worst time in my life, Ativan was the one thing that allowed me to keep going, to sleep and to get back to work, to be with my family until, like a bad weather system, the anxiety moved on. The pills made life endurable in a period when it often felt unendurable. As Solomon says, they can save lives. How much difference would it have made if my GP had prescribed Ativan, or Valium, or some other benzodiazepine to me? With a prescription, I could have gone to my only source of relief without fear or guilt. Instead, by making these drugs dangerous and illicit they became another motor for my anxiety.

I did have a prescription for the antidepressant venlafaxine, which I carried on taking every day – I still take it now, every morning after breakfast. It is a ritual, something I can do without thinking. I take a glass of water into the spare room, close the door, and get the packet from my desk drawer. The pills vary in appearance, depending on the manufacturer – circular, coral coloured, grooved down the middle, but other times darker, redder and smaller, like a multivitamin. Whatever the appearance, the pill has a bitter chemical taste which makes me gag and is hard to get rid of, so I am careful to wash it down quickly so that it doesn't touch the sides of my mouth. All this is so habitual that a minute or two later it is often hard to remember if I have actually done it. Like the Ativan, when I go away I check repeatedly that I have it, and stash spare strips in different places in case a bag gets lost, which it never has.

I do not deny taking it, if it comes up, but I do not advertise it either. Friends seem surprised when I mention it – they think all this is in the past – and maybe it makes them think of me a little differently. I dislike the need, every six weeks, to request a repeat prescription, to pick it up from the surgery and then take it to the pharmacist. It reminds me that in some sense I am dependent on it. I dislike, too, the appointment with the GP, every year or so, to review it. Again, it is a reminder. I have reduced my dose and at the appointment we usually discuss whether I might come off it altogether. The GP doesn't consider it essential that I stop. We have people on it for years, he says – and I guess I am now one of them. I say I will think about it, but I don't, or not for long.

Some people feel that taking medication like this alters them in a fundamental way, that it deadens them perhaps, or artificially brightens them, makes them a different person. They may or may not want that. I do not feel that way. I do not feel that it somehow distances me from my fundamental self. To me, anxiety is something like the malfunctioning of the human machine, like a broken thermostat, or a cog spinning loose in a gearbox – mechanical metaphors seem to present themselves. Perhaps this is why the word 'breakdown' is so ubiquitous, so enduring and so apt. You take a drug to fix the machine or to return you to yourself.

I do not think that the venlafaxine changes who I am but, from time to time, I do doubt my mood, the way I am feeling. It happens most often when I am walking in the woods with the dog or listening to music, and I experience a sudden rush or intensity of emotion, a high. I wonder, then, whether what I have just felt is not some authentic response to the moment but the result of the drug releasing itself into my bloodstream, or, more accurately, preventing the reabsorption of serotonin, norepinephrine and dopamine into my neurons. 'Which of my feelings are real?' wrote Kay Redfield Jamison, although she was talking about her illness itself, rather than the medication she took to control it.

I have no idea what effect the venlafaxine has, and it cannot be perfect because I still suffer from periods of anxiety. Since I have been on it I have not suffered a major relapse, but the two things may not be related. Perhaps it protects me from the extremes – it is impossible to know, except perhaps by coming off it. It is said to be hard to come off, even if you do it slowly and carefully, harder than other similar drugs, if you believe what is said on the forums, which report dizziness, headaches, vomiting, acute anxiety and depression. People often describe the sensation of little electric charges or shocks going off in the brain. But the short term is only part of what dissuades me. For coming off the pills, my GP advised choosing a period when I am unlikely to be experiencing any major stresses or change, but there is never a good time to risk a breakdown. I simply cannot contemplate the possibility, three months or six months or a year later, of unravelling as completely as I have done before; of not being able to sleep, or work, or write; of struggling to eat, or leave the house, or be with or without other people; of two years putting myself back together; of going back on the pills but discovering things have changed and now they don't help; of the moment-to-moment agony of consuming anxiety. Balanced against this, taking the pills long term feels like an easy decision to make.

2

A YEAR AFTER I HAD VIEWED THE NEW HOUSES AT the Kingswood Heath development I received an email alert from the company who had bought and converted the retained Severalls Hospital buildings. The largest of these had been one of the wards, in later years accommodating short-stay women at one end and short-stay men at the other. This was now named the Echelon Building, a reference to the original architectural design of the hospital as well as the particular zigzagging shape of the building's footprint, and had been turned into a terrace of seventeen houses. They were trailed on the developer's website as 'Homes with Grandeur' at 'A Refined Address'. None of my previous visits to the site had got me close to the hospital buildings themselves, let alone inside them. Here was my opportunity.

I took the train up to Colchester and arrived at Kingswood Heath with time to spare before my appointment. Earlier in the year, alongside seven other towns, Colchester had been granted city status to mark the Queen's Platinum Jubilee. A

great deal seemed to have changed on the ground here, too.
The development now spread over a vast area, beyond just
the original 300 acres of the hospital site, and had merged
with other adjacent developments. Roads of new housing
disappeared in every direction. Here and there, work was
still going on, foundations being dug, houses half built,
large vehicles and machinery, fencing, people in hard hats
and hi-vis, but the greater part of it seemed complete.

Only fragments of the old hospital remained, buried
deep in this new suburban landscape, and the effect was odd,
uncanny even. On my last visit the water tower was some
way off, inaccessible, deep into the fenced-off building site
and covered in scaffolding. Now the new housing spread all
the way up to it and the scaffolding was down. I stood at its
foot and looked up. It was a substantial red-brick building,
square and thick at the base, 100 feet high, plain and mono-
lithic. Three narrow, leaded windows were spaced evenly up
each side. Near the summit a modern glass and steel balcony
ran in a lip around the edge. I had read that the developers
of the retained buildings were turning this top floor into
their company office.

The imperatives of development and conservation
seemed to clash sharply here. The new builds paid lip service to the old hospital architecture, the use of red brick
and black stone, the height and shape of the windows, but
they stood much too close to the tower – by stretching out
my arms I could touch both at the same time – overlooked
and overshadowed. It seemed perverse to have retained this
landmark and then tried to crowd it out. Fixed to the side

of the tower was an information board titled 'Old Severalls Hospital', which provided a potted history of the place and photos of the hospital buildings as they had been. The board is informative up to a point, but it is notable that there is no mention of the words 'asylum' or 'mental hospital', and only a buried detail at the end to say it 'closed as a psychiatric hospital' in the 1990s.

Down the street and around the corner was the Administration Building, once the public face of the asylum, the point of entry for all new admissions. This was where my father had sat in 1968, in a wheelchair, and stared down the longest corridor in Europe into the interior of the hospital. On my first walk around the site I had seen it from a bank on the other side of the fence, the windows boarded up, the clock face cracked, the gutted contents of the interior piled up in front. Now the buildings that it had been connected to had gone but the Administration Building had retained its name and been converted into a single, 5,500-square-foot house, advertised as 'a fine example of the Queen Anne style... arguably Colchester's most impressive residence' and on the market for £1.35 million. Huge bays, five windows across, flanked an arched stone entrance which rose, above the second storey, to the repaired clock face, a sharply pitched roof and a stone cupola. The red brickwork had been cleaned up and repointed, the windows restored and repainted. To the left of the entrance, embedded in the wall, was the foundation stone of the hospital, 'laid by Sir Thomas Barrett-Lennard, Bart, of Belhus, Aueley, Essex, Chairman of the Committee of Visitors on the 21st day of June 1910'. There was no doubting its grandeur – and presumably it would sell – but shorn of its context, its power even, marooned in the middle of this sprawling modern estate, it struck the same dissonant note as the water tower, a curiosity, an odd and orphaned artefact.

The Administration Building stood at the head of a large circular drive, which I recognised from old pictures of the hospital. The drive encircled a freshly mown lawn, which was now being styled as a 'memorial garden', although it was just a modest patch of grass. At the centre of the lawn was a stone engraved with the names of fifteen hospital staff who had died in the First World War. On top of this was a metal plaque dedicated to the thirty-eight patients who had been killed in the German bombing in August 1942.

I met Ronan, the estate agent, outside the Echelon Building. He was young, mid-twenties I guessed, and friendly. We chatted easily and I felt none of the tension of my last visit. He had gone to a school near mine, in the middle of a large estate which had a reputation for being very rough. I told him that when I was at school in the 1980s there was always talk of rival gangs from our schools meeting at the big Tesco at lunchtimes to fight with bicycle chains and iron bars, although as far as I knew it had never actually happened. He laughed and said there had still been the same talk twenty years later.

The sun had come out and the scrubbed-clean red brick and freshly painted window frames of the long ter-race glowed warmly against the autumn sky. Ronan showed me four of the houses that were finished and still available. Another two were already occupied and the rest, at the far end of the building, were still being converted. The houses had three or four bedrooms but they were all very large and made to feel even bigger by the high ceilings – up to twelve feet in some places, according to the additional literature Ronan gave me. A corridor had once run the length of the building, and in partitioning it off all sorts of odd shapes and angles had been created.

This was the high end of the market, a different story to the generic new builds I had been inside on my last visit, where space and style had felt carefully rationed. Each house was individually designed, a different layout, a different combination of colours, materials and textures. The kitchens were fitted with top-of-the-range German appliances and the floors were some combination of polished concrete, engineered wood or, upstairs in the bedrooms, thick, springy carpet that we walked on in our socks. Original features had been kept. When the hospital was open, the huge sash windows were a problem because they provided ligature points for patients who wished to hang themselves. Now they had been refurbished and light flooded through them into the rooms. The living room and hallway in two of the houses were divided by vast sliding wooden doors painted aubergine purple. The wrought iron mechanism that allowed them to roll smoothly back and forth – Ronan encouraged me to have a go – had an almost medieval look but was, in fact, based on the original hospital doors and re-created by the developer. In the largest and most expensive of the houses, one of the original staircases had been kept, a massive institutional beast of concrete and original pockmarked tile work reimagined as contemporary design.

I stood at the bedroom window at the back of one of the houses and looked out. The gardens were tiny, a few feet of grass and gravel, and gave way immediately to the new houses that flowed up to and around the water tower and the Administration Building and beyond. 'The new homes have been designed to sit in harmony with the traditional character of the development' one of the brochures said, but it was hard to buy into this. The large-windowed, high-ceilinged Edwardian hospital building that I stood in now had been set into rolling parkland that would allow 'an uninterrupted view of surrounding country and free access of sun, and air'. I thought again of the playing fields, the farm, the laundry, the social club, the dance hall and the acres of beautifully kept gardens, so lovely that even my mother, in her unhappiness, could appreciate and find comfort in them. The Second Essex County Lunatic Asylum was designed to accommodate around 1,500 patients and 500 staff. The 1,000 new builds of Kingswood Heath will be home to vastly more people than that. The green spaces feel meagre, begrudging, and the reality is densely residential; there is the school and the David Lloyd gym and the football stadium, and there are plans for a Co-op, but as yet there are no shops, doctor's surgeries, cafes or pubs, or community spaces of any kind.

My feelings about Severalls were complicated. There were handsome buildings but there were also comfortless and, at one time, crowded wards. It was not a spa hotel or holiday camp. It was a place where people were sent and kept, sometimes against their will, sometimes for their own benefit and sometimes not, and where, as well as care and treatment, there was abuse and neglect. I should not lament it. But I could not help but regret the erasure of the past. There was the foundation stone, the small memorials to the staff killed in the First World War and the patients killed in the Second, the information board fastened to the water tower, but all this was very easy to miss – the thin, hard-won gains of community groups against the onslaught of development and capital. I regretted, too, the larger social truth it represented, that despite the PR homilies of government policy documents, over the last fifty years public responsibility for the mentally ill has been drastically and disastrously eroded. 'A façade of care concealing a black hole of neglect,' writes Mike Jay of the palatial new Bethlem built at Moorfields in 1676, and the same could be said of mental health provision nearly 350 years later. The reality is that cash-strapped local authorities and NHS Trusts have sold off public resources and land to private developers, and the trappings of these visionary, deeply flawed institutions have been turned into aspirational lifestyle details.

Ronan locked up the final house and offered me a lift to the station. I thanked him but said I would walk. He told me to get in touch if I was still interested in the houses and then got in his car and drove off. Unlike the rear view, the front of the houses looked onto an area of communal land that spread to the outer perimeter of the development and the main road. In the literature this was referred to as 'The Echelon Wood', 'landscaped with mature trees and planting… a haven of green and calm'. This was overstating it, as ever. There were few trees and the ground was still churned into mud from trucks and diggers, but Ronan had assured me this would all be turfed and planted in due course. At intervals amongst the mud were 'summer shelters', white wooden structures, roofed over but open at the sides, with benching underneath, like something you might find on a seaside promenade. The ones that stood here now were re-creations of the originals, which had been bulldozed in an early phase of the redevelopment. When the hospital was open they had been a place for staff and patients to sit and admire the grounds, take in the air or shelter from the rain or the sun. 'A haven of green and calm': the language still seems rooted in the old ideal. Perhaps my father had sat in one of these shelters and watched my mother putt balls across the green when he was a patient, or they were somewhere my mother came and sat, later, when she was a patient herself.

I took a paved path across the mud and sat down in one of the shelters. For me, the old Severalls site had always stood for more than just a social truth. My interest in it was never neutral. For as long as I had known about it, Severalls had been a place of mystery and dread. It was a place that had done nothing – at least nothing good – for either of my parents, a place which had taken my mother away and where she had suffered. Haunted is too strong a word, perhaps, but I had felt the pull of the place, a kind of magnetism.

Despite the first trip to the site with my parents, I made the subsequent visits without telling anyone and without thinking clearly about my motives. I felt what I had been doing might be difficult to justify – or merely silly, a waste of time, meaningless. It was easier not to articulate it precisely, or look it in the eye. When I had become ill, as I lay awake on the sofa in our flat in the middle of the night, convinced, suddenly, that I was losing my mind, my first instinct was that I needed to be in hospital, somewhere – I suppose – like Severalls. In truth, what I wanted was just to be looked after, cared for, for someone to take responsibility for me, to hand myself over. I was lucky that I had family and friends to do that. I did not end up in hospital but I felt, nevertheless, that I had crossed some kind of threshold. My parents had crossed this threshold far more comprehensively, and what I wanted, I think now, was to try to understand – or at least try to imagine – a little more of what my mother and father, separately and together, had been through in these difficult years: the loneliness and desperation, the sense of life veering off course. I had felt this acutely about my own life, for a time, and it seemed like it might all be part of the same story.

Severalls was symbolic of all this, and my visits – and my reading and research – were a clunky, blind probing at what was there. The metaphor seems too easy perhaps, too convenient, but by circling the hospital, penetrating the grounds and, finally, entering its buildings I was pushing into the hidden rooms of my own past. Each time I went I was hoping for some kind of friction, a reaction, a revelation. Only it did not happen – not really. Objects, people and places gain power and magnetism from remaining obscure, out of reach, unknown. My imagination had poured into the gap between my idea of the place and my experience of it but each time I went to Severalls, each thing I read about it, the smaller that gap became, the weaker its pull on me. Dread and monstrosity were replaced by complexity and ambivalence.

A family had come out of one of the houses in the Echelon Building, a man and a woman a little younger than me, and a toddler. They stood on the doorstep whilst the father pulled a top down over the child's head. The woman started to water some plants in pots by the door. I had wanted to judge this place, perhaps even the people in it, to find it wanting in some way, but I no longer had the heart for it. Perhaps the family on the doorstep knew the history of the building they were living in and perhaps they didn't. It made no difference. The houses would all be sold. The grass would grow and the mud would disappear. The summer shelters would age and weather until no one would be able to tell that they were only reproductions of the originals. People would live here and get to know their neighbours and raise their kids and call it home.

Over the next few days I expected a call from Ronan, to follow up on our appointment, but it never came.

3

THERE IS NOT MUCH TO BE SAID IN FAVOUR OF mental illness. It is life-wrecking, life-ending, for many. On average in the UK, people with severe and prolonged mental illness die fifteen to twenty years earlier than the general population. The notion of it as a sane reaction to an insane world, a kind of burden of truth, has the strong whiff of ideology and does not bear much contact with the reality of suffering or caring for someone who is suffering.

My own experience of mental illness has been in a minor key. I could not know this at the time but my breakdown was not the beginning of a long trek into the further, more chaotic realms of psychological distress; or at least it would not seem to be. I have not been psychotic, except briefly and under specific conditions in intensive care. I never harmed anyone or tried to harm myself. I did not end up addicted to tranquillizers. It troubled but did not destroy my personal or professional life. Instead I got better, slowly. With the support of family, friends, employers and the illicit pills that Chris gave me, I got through it. In the long term it has not limited me, or not a great deal. I have been able to live normally and write about it, with an enduring sense of the alternative histories that might have panned out for me. It was the worst, most defining experience of my life by far, and yet I know that it could have been far worse. Perhaps it would be reasonable to say I have dodged that bullet.

Poor mental health has dogged my parents' lives. After his time in Severalls, my father continued to suffer from anxiety but managed to carry on working. He did not enjoy being an academic and wanted to leave the university but was afraid his health might not hold up. Nevertheless, in 1987, at the age of forty-six, he took redundancy and went to teach at the newly opened sixth form college in Colchester, the beginning of a second, much more rewarding career. Following the treatment for chronic fatigue in his late sixties, his health improved but the fear of a relapse remained powerful.

My mother's health was more volatile and in later years the manic pole of her illness asserted itself more fully. In 2000 she saw her medical notes and learned that she had been given the label 'bipolar disorder', the first time she had heard this diagnosis. She recovered from the breakdown that put her into Severalls and the Royal Free and started working as a secretary in a grammar school. My parents began their jobs at the college and the school on the same day and it must have felt like a new beginning. My mother enjoyed the job and was good at it, but in 1990 she began another cycle of mania and depression which eventually led to her early retirement in 1997. Another manic period followed in

2000, but she gradually came down from it and began the most sustained period of good health since the 1970s.

In *A Farewell to Arms*, Ernest Hemingway wrote, 'The world breaks everyone and afterward many are strong at the broken places.' I came across this line when I was ill, posted on an anxiety forum somewhere, and even then it seemed insincere, fanciful. Now though, if I have understood it correctly, I think it is exactly wrong, something that should not have got past the 'built-in bullshit detector' Hemingway said was necessary for all writers. There is another phrase, which you hear all the time, something from Nietzsche: whatever doesn't kill you makes you stronger. They are both wishful thinking, sentimental, a little macho, articulating the myth of growth through suffering. Whatever doesn't kill you might still weaken you in the long run. The places where you have been broken remain your structural weaknesses, the places most likely to bend, or crumble or snap under the strain.

A few months ago, I thought it might be happening again. I woke up dizzy, a little nauseous, with no appetite. I had an all-day meeting online and as the hours passed, trapped on screen, the feeling escalated. I began to read the signs and then read them again, finding the evidence: the impossibility of making the smallest decisions, the sense of paralysis, the dizziness, the nausea. But it is not so much how you feel at those moments as how you know it is possible to feel, where this ends up, the fear of what's coming. You have been there before and cannot unknow that and your mind travels ahead, writing the script, fulfilling itself. You remember the other times when things were desperate

– vomiting on a beach in Dorset, sitting in the GP's office, awake at 4 a.m. day after day.

Everything looks different at times like this: that the period of stable mental health and relative equilibrium is not, in fact, the norm, the natural or fundamental state, but itself a kind of glitch, the calm between storms. The narrative of illness begins to reassert itself and it seems possible – and of course it is possible – that the collapse of my early thirties was not the final destination but just another staging post, like the migraines of my childhood and the fatigue of my twenties, on the way to something worse. I think, inevitably, of my father and the chronic fatigue that blighted his retirement.

Thoughts circle and catastrophise. The structures of normal life seem suddenly at risk and you see how they might all be stripped away – the ability to work, to be with family, to see friends – and an abyss opens up below. For several days I felt myself teetering on the brink, the possibility of a full unravelling. I took Ativan to make sure I slept at night and thought about asking for more from Chris. I took the venlafaxine with increased deliberateness, and when I was out I fretted that I had forgotten to take it at all. Everything felt precarious, heightened, fragile. And, having forgotten how awful this is, or nearly is, and how I would give anything not to feel this way, I vowed, as I had before, that once the moment passed – if it passed – this time I would not forget or be complacent about what it means to feel well. But then the crisis does pass and after a few weeks I do forget, more or less, because it is not possible to live like this, and, after all, complacency is a form of happiness.

Ellie and I avoid talking about my time in intensive care in front of the children. If other people bring it up, we shush them or change the subject. Around two years after I was in hospital my daughter had a series of panic attacks. If I was late home from work or took longer at the shops than planned, she quickly became anxious, hysterical. At the time I was reluctant to accept a straightforward connection to my illness, the weeks when it seemed that I might die, the sight of me unconscious in intensive care. Perhaps I did not want to feel responsible for her distress, although it was obvious to Ellie then, and obvious to me now. My daughter had some counselling and the panic attacks went away.

We do not talk, either, about my anxiety, how unwell I felt when my daughter was small and before my son was born. Perhaps, it occurs to me now, I am replicating the pattern of my parents – the desire not to speak about difficult things, to move on, to obscure or omit. But it is not – like everything – as simple as that. There is a conflict between healthy openness and the desire to maintain some kind of innocence. My children are still young and it seems too much, unnecessary to their lives. Parents make these sorts of decisions every day, in smaller ways – turning the radio down or the television off when the news is distressing, steering a child quickly past a dead bird on the street. It is easier, anyway, to write about all this than to talk about it. I have written this and perhaps one day, when they are older, my children will read it.

I wonder, of course, about what I might have passed on to them over the long term, through genes or behaviour or exposure to traumatic events. It is natural, as a parent, to want to model some kind of happiness, to protect them from the knowledge or experience of suffering. Over the years I have sometimes thought about what it would have been like to grow up without my mother if she had not survived the worst of her illness. It is hard, too, when I am feeling morbid or sentimental, not to picture my family without me, several years down the line from intensive care, when they have adapted, my son so young that he has no memory of me at all. Imaginative doors are opened by these things and sometimes my mind disappears through them. Perhaps my daughter's does, too. I worry about the bullet, whether it will find them and what pain it might cause.

We pass these things on, but we pass on other things, too – love, care, understanding. I think of what my parents survived together, and all they have done for my brother and me. When I was ill my mother came to see me and talked about the day she and I walked around Ullswater whilst my father and brother rowed across the lake to meet us. I cannot place this holiday exactly. We went to the Lake District many times, but I think it would have been before she became ill in 1984. Perhaps it – the walk, the lake, my father and brother rowing to meet us – was an image, a memory, she had once clung to herself in difficult times. She knew how to console me because she had once consoled herself. 'That was a happy day,' she said. 'That was a happy day.'

Bibliography

THIS IS, AT HEART, A PERSONAL STORY AND THROUGH-
out the writing of the book I have been very aware that
I am not a historian, sociologist or medical professional.
As such, I have relied on the work of a large number of
writers, academics, clinicians and other experts to inform
my understanding of psychiatric illness and its treatment
in the UK and elsewhere. In particular, I could not have
written the book without Diana Gittins' fascinating and
unique study of Severalls Hospital, *Madness in its Place*.
The archived research materials for the book held at the
Wellcome Collection were also invaluable. Barbara Taylor's
extraordinary *The Last Asylum* was an early and continual
source of inspiration and a model for what I wanted to do.

Listed below is a range of sources that I quote directly in
the book or which provided vital context and background.

Appignanesi, Lisa, *Mad, Bad and Sad: A History of Women
and the Mind Doctors from 1800 to the Present* (Virago,
2009)

Barham, Peter, *Closing the Asylum: The Mental Patient in Modern Society* (Penguin, 1992)

Barton, Russell, *Institutional Neurosis* (John Wright & Sons, 1976)

Bedlam, Channel 4, 31 October–21 November 2013

Dillon, Brian, *Tormented Hope: Nine Hypochondriac Lives* (Penguin, 2010)

Fitzgerald, F. Scott, *The Crack-Up* (New Directions, 1993)

Foot, John, *The Man Who Closed the Asylums: Franco Basaglia and the Revolution in Mental Health Care* (Verso, 2015)

Foucault, Michel, *Madness and Civilization* (Routledge, 2001)

Gittins, Diana, *Madness in its Place: Narratives of Severalls Hospital, 1913–1997* (Routledge, 1998)

Goffman, Erving, *Asylums* (Penguin, 1991)

Jay, Mike, *This Way Madness Lies: The Asylum and Beyond* (Thames & Hudson/Wellcome Collection, 2016)

Jamison, Kay Redfield, *An Unquiet Mind: A Memoir of Moods and Madness* (Picador, 1997)

Jamison, Kay Redfield, *Touched with Fire: Manic-Depressive Illness and the Artistic Temperament* (Macmillan, 1993)

Kesey, Ken, *One Flew Over the Cuckoo's Nest* (Viking, 1962)

Laing, R. D., *The Divided Self* (Penguin, 2010)

One Flew Over the Cuckoo's Nest, dir. by Miloš Forman (United Artists, 1975)

O'Sullivan, Suzanne, *It's All in Your Head: True Stories of Imaginary Illness* (Vintage, 2016)

Plath, Sylvia, *The Bell Jar* (Faber, 2001)

Porter, Roy, ed., *The Faber Book of Madness* (Faber, 1991)

Solomon, Andrew, *The Noonday Demon: An Anatomy of Depression* (Vintage, 2002)

Sutherland, Stuart, *Breakdown: A Personal Crisis and a Medical Dilemma* (OUP, 1998)

Styron, William, *Darkness Visible: A Memoir of Madness* (Picador, 1991)

Szasz, Thomas, *The Myth of Mental Illness* (Harper Perennial, 2010)

Taylor, Barbara, *The Last Asylum: A Memoir of Madness in Our Times* (Penguin, 2014)

Tone, Andrea, *The Age of Anxiety: A History of America's Turbulent Affair with Tranquilizers* (Basic Books, 2009)

Weekes, Claire, *Self-Help for Your Nerves* (Angus & Robertson, 1977)

Wolpert, Lewis, *Malignant Sadness: The Anatomy of Depression* (Faber, 1999)

The County Asylums website (www.countyasylums.co.uk) is a superb resource and provided invaluable information on Severalls and the rest of the asylum network.

Various reports by The King's Fund (www.kingsfund.org.uk) provided useful detail and statistics on mental health policy and provision.

Acknowledgements

WRITING NON-FICTION HAS TURNED OUT TO BE both much more fraught and much more collaborative than just making things up, and I have depended on a large number of people for help of all kinds.

Huge thanks and credit are due to Laura Barber, my editor, for belief in the original idea, considerable patience and understanding during the writing and, most crucially, her brilliant and sensitive editorial vision. I couldn't have asked for more.

Thank you to everyone else at Granta for once again making it the best possible place to be, in particular Christine Lo, Jack Alexander and Pru Rowlandson (in anticipation!). Thank you to Jonathan Pelham for the bold and amazing cover.

The beginnings of the book lie in two essays written for Brendan Barrington at *The Dublin Review*, 'The Creaking Door' and 'The Invader and the Antidote'. A third piece, 'My Father's Asylum', was also published in the *Review* at a crucial moment in the book's development. Brendan's support and forensic edits have been crucial to me as a writer since he published my first story twenty years ago.

A number of friends and fellow writers read the manuscript at different stages and provided invaluable encouragement and insight: Josh Cohen, Ben Crewe, Maura Dooley, Sophie Hardach, Nell Stevens, Jenny Worton. Particular thanks are due to Alistair Daniel for his meticulous and perceptive readings (of this and everything else). For valuable conversations about the current state of mental health services, many thanks to Dr Emily Baker, Dr Joe Hall and Dr Rebecca Moore.

Over the last few years I have benefited from the generous support of the Royal Literary Fund and I am very grateful to Steve Cook and the rest of the team there. A grant from the Society of Authors helped fund the early stages of writing the book. I am also very grateful for the support and good humour of all my colleagues in the Department of English and Creative Writing at Goldsmiths.

Thank you to genius agent Cathryn Summerhayes for making everything happen and for replying to emails almost before I've sent them.

And finally, and most of all, thanks and love to my family – Lees, de Zoysas and Lee de Zoysas. Thank you for encouraging, participating in, studiously ignoring or being completely uninterested in what I was doing. I needed it all.